W9-BJU-842

ARTEMISION

IDYLLS AND SONGS

ARTEMISION

IDYLLS AND SONGS

BY

MAURICE HEWLETT

Μέλλον ἄρα στυγερὰν κἀγώ ποτε δῆριν Ἄρηος
    ἐκπρολιποῦσα χορῶν παρθενίων ἀΐειν
Ἀρτέμιδος περι ναόν,...

ANTHOL, II., 29

NEW YORK

CHARLES SCRIBNER'S SONS

153-157, FIFTH AVENUE

M CM IX

821
H49

First Published . . *April* 1909

PR
4787
A7
1909

DEDICATION

I WILL make an altar of earth
With myrtle deckt and with yew,
Covered with sods : the dew
Shall wash it dainty and clean.
I raise it, O Child, to you ;
To the peace you have, and the mirth,
To the wells of love in your eyes
And the sweet tide of your breath,
To your young blood ere it dries ;
To Innocence, Ardour, and You.

Hymnia you shall be call'd ;
For worship of you the shrine
Is built of pure thought, and fine
As the mould of your shapeliness.
Let Summer breathe on it, and bees,
And the wind's love ; from the vine
I borrow clinging ; let Dawn
Greet you thro' lattice of trees—
Plane, and Poplar that sighs,
And Lime, the lover of bees.

Smooth, rounded, and knit
As the fashion of perfect limbs
I would have it be : of your eyes
I ask for the sanctities

1/27/47 W. Wilson
76944

Of their violet glint ere it dims,
To kindle the fire on it.
Above the green altar-ledge
Still, incessant, your eyes
Fire the dusk : they are lit
From the love in my heart that lies.

Give of your hair to hide
The altar-house ; spray it wide
In a silk mesh—ah, my pride !
Was ever iconostase
So superbly bedeckt
With warm brown curtain, or fleckt
As this with rays of the sun ?
Or when since Mass was begun
Came priest to cover his face
In so burnisht curtain and wide ?

Your breath is for incense-flight
From the censer pure of your mouth :
It is odorous of the South
And the pastures of all the West.
The wet fresh growth of the year,
Honeysuckle and thyme,
Anemones meek as death,
Crocuses yellow and white :
All shy blossoms are here
Nurst in your balmy breath.

For altar-stone is your lap
Whereon, a pure offering,

Dedication

I lay down flowers, a song,
A bird's dropt feather, a ring
Woven of scented rush
For my spousal with Earth. And I crush
From mallows the milky sap,
Flour from the burnt brown wheat,
And from limes the honey, to make
For the altar a fairy cake.

Kneeling, I lift eyes up
The ripple of you, and see
As a bud stiff on her stalk
Your face in whose beam I walk
Lift from your gown's dark cup,
And your grave eyes fixt on me.
Then I fall, bending the knee,
For your mouth quivers, a tear
Veils your seeing : I know
Your heart's grief, O my dear !

Heaven kiss'd Earth and loved her
Face to face in the wild
Still deeps of a night
Once in June. O Child,
Thou, pledge of delight,
Thou wert born of that night,
Spirit of Earth, the joy
Of whoso loveth cool rain,
And summer heats, and the pain
Of frosts, and spring's onset mild :—
Thou art Earth's quick-born child !

1895.

CONTENTS

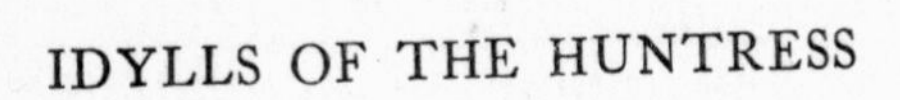

IDYLLS OF THE HUNTRESS

LETO'S CHILD

SING first (but in the rustic mood)
Arcady's grassy solitude ;
The billowing hills, the woods and brakes,
The plains, the streams, the rushy lakes,
Where haunts the Spirit of all that wild,
Virgin and Huntress, Leto's child,
Under the quiet name she has
Of Hymnia, the Gentle Shepherdess.

She those wide pastures scared by Pan
Roameth unwatcht of any man,
Save of the wondering herd-boy lying
Betwixt his fires, who by the dying
Flicker sees her (with fearful breath)
Within the cote draw quick from death
And in her bosom hide the lamb
Newborn, and still the moaning dam.
Or sometimes, ere the morning gold
Layeth its slant warmth on the wold,
In that murk twilight hour he sees
Her fleeting by him with bare knees
And streaming tresses, light and fierce,
Hounding her hounds ; or sometimes hears
Her voice ring up the sleeping hills
Like the dawn wind that keens and shrills
About the valleys. But all day

The uplands know her not. Her way
Is with the creatures wild and shy
Darkling in coverts, where they lie
Till thickest night come, and the hour,
That all men charmeth and men's power,
Leaves earth the fee of beast and bird.

Unseen by eyes, by ears unheard
Of men grown old and satiate
In ways where clamour keeps the gate!
But seen by him who, having prayed
Awhile, takes heart to sing this Maid.
Ah, Maiden of all maids for him
Since first she glimmered sweet and dim
Before him in the falling haze
Late, at the parting of the ways,
And looking on him with great eyes
Full of light, served to imparadise
His earth-born soul, and made clean song
Break flowerlike from his lips and strong;
And made it his to tell her worth
Whose breath from Heaven doth sweeten Earth.

Upon that time when a great calm
Gave Leto peace beneath the palm—
Her crutch and warrant of emprise
When she gave light to Heaven's two eyes—
Long years in Delos, harboured fast
Under the shadow Cynthus cast,
She watched her babes, and paid no fee
To any, but went solved and free

From sight of bird or beast or man ;
For all that coast lay under ban
Of Father Zeus, and all the seas
Were hushed that laved the Cyclades
While her truce lasted.
                                        Joy she took
In them, this woman man-forsook :
To see their growth keep comely pace
With the new-dawning God, and trace
The God-shine solemn in their eyes.
Pride of estate is hers, who lies
To dream her dreams ! Ah, but her pain
Who, waking, marks the chasm gain
Between her lowly griefs and that
Immortal ease she wonders at ;
And waits the moment of the break
Between her life and theirs, to take
Them lightly to a larger air
And leave her dark in her despair !
Here she lay down in arms with Sorrow
And nightlong wept ; but on the morrow,
Ere the full day, she stooped and yearned
Over them sleeping ; and one turned
A rosy face blowsed all with sleep
Up to her, and a smile 'gan creep—
As hill-tops kindle at sunrise
When the warm light awakes and flies :
Then no more anguish was for her
That day. So year by happy year
Sped Leto, feeding on her joy ;
And still she deemed them girl and boy

Who now, in youth's more hazardous lines
And soberer gait, stood like young pines
That on the hillside, curtseying
Before the gale, resilient swing
And shake their banners to the sun.
  But seeing at last her life-work done,
And instant theirs, this mother meek
Called them, and stilled her voice to speak
Against her tears ; and thus she said :
  'O dear desire and comelihead,
  'Wherein my Lord hath made my state
  'Above all mothers' fortunate !
  'Not so wise mother should I prove
  'If my own love should drown my love
  'Of that I live to love. Not mine
  'Your ways henceforward. Nay, untwine
  'Your close arms ; beating heart and heart,
  'Throb no accord with mine. Depart,
  'O Daughter, go you now, my Son.
  'Lo, ye are Gods ! I am not one.
  'Yet since no shame can make you less,
  'Nor harm come there where mothers bless
  'Their children—since they bless by prayer—
  'Kneel you this last time.'
                On their hair,
On heads submiss her hands she set
Tremulous, peering through her wet
Dim eyes unto the silver sea,
As if to search what cloud-wrapt fee
Would claim them : they, with folded hands
Couchéd for mercies, and the strands

Of their loose hair about their cheeks,
Like Caryatids bent. She speaks,
She lifts them to her, and in arms
Catches, and mutters age-old charms
To ward off evil, and call on
The kindly spirits. First her Son,
Loxias our Lord, within that nest
Haveneth ; then her she loves the best,
Hymnia the maiden pure, she makes
Lie on her bosom ; her heart aches
To feel that young heart leap for her
So fast, and those young lips astir
Against her mouth. She holds her head,
Half amorously and half in dread,
Between her two hands, gazing long
In her grey eyes ; then growing strong
To speak, whispers,
'Thou Holy One,
'By that pure face, by that pure zone,
'By all my mother-pains and bliss,
'Mother thou mothers, Artemis !
'Yea, tho' not love of god or youth
'Ripen thy breasts or draw thy mouth
'To need another's mouth or breast,
'And tho' not Thou mayst feel the blest
'Mother-estate, show all such grace !'
She spake, then, crouching, hid her face.

But those Two left the sanctuary
Of olives by the wine-dark sea
With wingèd Hermes, fixt and keen

To hail their birth-right : She to green
Arcadia, and the shouldering downs,
Where hide the little roughcast towns
Of country folk, and dense woodland
Brimmeth the valleys on each hand ;
And He a further course to set
For Phocian Delphi, and the fret
Parnassus makes, that twi-crown'd hill,
Whence leapeth musically the rill
Castaly, clear and strong as wine.
There tended him the Virgin Nine,
And there we leave him, following
Artemis to her home-bringing.
  Say, how did Cypris, wet from the sea,
Shine on Cythera ? Wistfully,
As tender of her welcome there
Who should bring pain and should bring care
As well as flame-red passion-flowers !
Therefore she chose the still dawn hours,
When wing'd Sleep brooded, on to glide,
Veiling her breasts and naked side
With her dank hair. But Artemis
Coursed swiftly home down winds that hiss
And blench the fretty-edged surf,
And drive cloud-shadows o'er the turf.
She chose that fresh cold wind and clear
That snows the forehead of the year
And sings an anthem sharp : a breeze
Out of the North-West drove white seas
And Her to sand-dunes, trees wind-torn
(Both red-heart willow and stubb'd thorn)

And wide sea-grasses stretching far.
By that swept shore a country car
Waited her, having two red deer
Yoked to the pole ; and charioteer
A maiden grave and tall there stood,
Clad in warm russet, with a hood
Of scarlet wool ; who held the reins
And goad, and scann'd the windy plains
Thro' the grey weather, till she 'scried
Her whom all waited for ; then cried
'Artemis ! Pæan !' and lit down
To kiss the border of her gown.
But Hymnia did bud her lips, and kiss'd her
Upon the cheek, as she were sister ;
And after, sisterly, hand in hand,
They two quitted that wild sea-strand,
Blown by the gale and salt sea-spray
(So that their hair did point the way),
'Twixt rustling sedges and bent flags.
Good speed and passage made the stags
Thro' the wide reaches of the marsh,
Where peewits wail'd and herons harsh
Flapt heavily to sea-ward.
Soon
They crosst the inmost ridge of dune,
And found green country, heard the roar
Of ocean faint, and what wind tore
Among the weather bents. Thereby
The great clouds mustered silently ;
And there, where tardily a stream
Coil'd thro' the meadows, and a gleam

Of sunlight warmed its eddies brown
And burnisht its slow surges, down
The sleepy pastures came a troop
Of maidens, clustering in a group
Of that same tawny tipt with red.
Each had bare feet, bare arms, bare head,
And all their tresses blown about
In clouds ; who, nearing, 'gan to lout
And curtsey, calling with one voice,
'Pæan to Artemis ! Rejoice,
'Ye heathen folk !' And one knelt down,
The ruddiest, offering her a crown
Made of wild parsley and thin grass ;
And she, Callisto her name was,
Who blusht the welcome of them all
Was slight as Hymnia, and as tall,
But bosom'd less, and much more shy,
Being unsteel'd by Deity—
Save that unconscious godlihead
A virgin hath before she wed ;
In whom a mystery unperturb'd
Keeps her eyes wide, but her lips curb'd.
Now as she knelt there looking up,
Timidly bright, the car did stop ;
Artemis lit, and all those round her
Knelt, and Callisto came and crown'd her
On her bent head, then shrill'd the chant
That still the Arcadian glens doth haunt :
'Pæan ! Pæan ! O Hymnia !
'Hail, Guarded Lips ! Hail, Maiden Fear !'
From Hymnia's face auroral hue

Answer'd ; and pansies glos'd with dew
Had not the lustre of her eyes ;
Nor ever thro' such sanctities
Of quivering lip and mantled cheek
Cried a storm'd heart the grace to speak.
(She was full young for this high honour,
And queenship thrust so soon upon her :
For even as day breaks falteringly,
So is the god-dawn faint and shy.)
But praise inflames, and when her pride
Flooded her and show'd glorified
The crown upon her brows, all knew
Their Queen was here ; in order due
They stood, and Hymnia held the ground
Betwixt them staidly—a child crown'd,
And led them then and ever.
Fast
They sped thro' deepening valleys, cast
In shade of beechen woods and groves
Of leafy oaks, made quick by droves
Of dappled deer that side by side
Stood wondering on her with eyes wide
And blinking ears. Beside her car
Her maidens cours'd in emulous war
Who should be nearest, so her gaze
Should first glad her who first should raise
Her waiting face ; but by her side,
Her mate, Callisto now did ride ;
On whose bare shoulders lightly stay'd
The God's young hand ; 'twixt whose eyes play'd
Love-urgencies of girl for girl,

Tremulously, as when the swirl
Of crossing currents sways drown'd things
To swift caresses, sunderings,
As works the stream's strong underflow.
 The mountains stand before them now,
Thigh-deep in forest, raising gaunt
Their scarr'd grey flanks, where Oreads haunt,
And Satyrs leap for Pan, or chase
The eye-bright Nymphs ; where lax vines lace
The jutty rocks, and silver shows
The mist of olives, red the rose
Upon the lower slopes ; but higher
The rowans cense the day with fire,
Where on the ridge in ragged lines
Stand, sombre hierophants, the pines,
Adoring heaven's blue vault. Hereby
Steep Erymanthus with the sky
Holds rapt communion, and not far
Mænalus, lone Cyllené are,
Whose splinter'd pikes and summits fell
More mysteries keep than tongue dare tell :
For here untrammell'd Hymnia moves
In the deep peace her spirit loves.
Sanctuary here ! let no man's foot
Be set, nor mannish eye take note
How she may bare her breast of snows
In the deep peace her plane-tree throws,
Menelaïs, mid hanging woods.
 Here an eternal silence broods,
Silence primeval, dim and vast.
Here stays her car, for she is fast

Leto's Child

In Arcady, and her demesne
Islanded in this lake of green
And rustling leaves. Beside this mount
Her precinct is, her shrine and fount,
Where, boled and brancht with silver age,
Her deep retreat and harbourage,
Menelaïs, the plane-tree, stands.
    Now on her bosom cross her hands.
Now let her bend her down until
Her kissing lips touch the clear rill
That down the hill-side droppeth slowly,
Sacrosanct, murmuring, lustral, holy ;
Whose waters well'd up in that night
When God said, 'Bless'd in all men's sight
'Art thou, Delos,' and it stood fast,
After long wanderings moored at last ;
Water more pure than ever hides
Callirrhoë for Attic brides,
More bright than aught that dyes her lips
When Arethuse Alphæus clips
(Rewarded for his burrowing) :
And when the Goddess set herein
Her two white hands, and urged her sweet
Lips till they met their counterfeit,
Beauty with Beauty kiss'd, and strove
Which should kiss last ; and the moon wove
To hold the pair a silver frame.
Thus to her Arcady she came.

    And now those leafy silent glens,
And those brown hillsides and great fens,

That guard the river with their hedge
Of feather'd reed and watersedge,
Were stirred as with an undersense
Of a not seen yet quick Presence.
Now shepherds, coucht beside their fires
Under the stars, heard hidden choirs
Of shrill girl-voices rise and fall
From hill to hill—call answering call ;
Heard flying feet or panting breath ;
Or saw a stricken stag find death
Where none was by to deal the wound
With bow or spear-shaft. Or one found,
When to his darken'd hut he hied
And wife in travail, stoopt beside
The bed a Lady bright, who drew
The babe into her mantle blue
And to her bosom prest it. One
Stood near her, fair to look upon,
But watching with intent dog's eyes
That fairer nurse. And soon the cries
Were low in mother and in child,
And both at rest. Which done, she smiled
Upon her handmaid, and both past
Out of the door and made it fast,
Silently, going as they came.
And in the cotes it was the same
As under the brown eaves. O' night
In winter-time, when all in white
The world lay dully, she would pass
Trackless upon the frozen grass
To rid the burthen'd ewes, and draw

The lambs within the shealing straw
And wattles. She too from the flocks
Past to their bane, the sly bitch-fox,
And to her sandy earth brought peace.
The squirrels quick that nest in trees,
The lightfoot deer, that in the glades
Go twitching ears and skuts, she aids ;
The hare that loves the corn and furrow,
The huddled coney deep in burrow,
The company of birds—all things
That breathe partook her ministerings ;
And in her motions free and light,
And swift, down-searching, inward sight,
Knew of a truth (as One should tell
Later) Who markt what sparrows fell.
Thus she was Gentle Shepherdess,
Because she stooped to things in stress,
And mother'd things that scarce draw breath,
And saved by life or saved by death.
Therefore on oaten pipes or flutes
The shepherds quired her attributes,
And nam'd her Hymnia, boon and calm,
In prayer and thanksgiving and psalm.

Hear ye now whither Fortune drove
That nymph Callisto, who in love
Was chiefest of her maids, whose part
Drew her to rest by Hymnia's heart—
For sleep not sever'd them, but one
Was to the other as a sun
That hangs attendant on a star,

And takes and lends her light afar,
For whom such love as She—proud Lover—
Could for the Earth-born she gave over
With courtesy and humour sweet
That is not love, nor counterfeit
Of love, but as a garment worn
For festival, points the high-born.
Thus one was lover, and one let
Herself be lov'd with eyes unwet.
Chian or Mantuan, succour me!
To tell how they beneath the tree,
Thick Menelaïs, lay and talkt
The drowsy noon away, or walkt,
Linkt by the waist, the long grass rides,
Under the oaks, or by the sides
Of brawly rivers racing down
Foam-fleckt; or, when She doff'd her gown
And stood up pure in all her sweet
Bare beauty gleaming in the heat,
How watcht Callisto lest some shame
Should dare come near: none ever came.
Or how on sand and pebbles cool
Lay Hymnia, white and wonderful,
And let the amorous water glide
Over her shoulders, down her side,
And kiss her here and there. Nor long
Callisto left her. Soon among
The lipping waves she too stretcht out,
And gave and took the same sweet bout.
Or their commerce, half love, half sport;
As when two not own'd lovers court

And tease each other, but betray
By panting what is not all play.
Too close the Nymph did play, too clear
Her heart-beats let her heart appear
To one who such earth-love knew not,
Nor guess'd what made this friend so hot
To cling and kiss. That crying need
The earth-born have (whose hearts must bleed
To cool their surfeit fires) she past
Unheeded, ignorantly chaste,
As upland peaks that wear the white
Of brides, yet keep their lone delight.
And if (provok'd to 't) She'd begin
To play in turn, hold up her chin
With two slim fingers, and look down
Unto that breathing mouth, those brown
Deep eyes that in their mirror gave
Herself again, Callisto clave
Closer to this her graver mate,
With pamper'd love insatiate
(As a fed horse that shakes the bit
And finds a spur, not curb, in it) ;
Requiring love as fierce and close
As that she offer'd. Not as those
Maidens on earth seek each their lad,
Half shy, half welcoming, all glad,
Lookt up Callisto, but to crave
More kindnesses than she might have.
As craved Evadne when she crept
To her lord's pyre, and burning slept
Body by body, ash with ash—

So loved Callisto hot and rash ;
For whom, as Love grew to be master,
Her needs to pay his scot cried, Faster !
  Ah, passion of the wound so wide
  No balm may fill it, no scar hide—
  Passion that drains the love-denied !
For lo, the more the Nymph did dote
The Goddess colder, more remote
Went guarded. As in her own tears
Dircè lives on dissolv'd, whose fears
Froze ere they thaw'd her, so love-gladness
Burnt pleasure in her mouth to madness
For Hymnia's hoarded lips and eyes.
Refused, Callisto storms, she cries,
Sits much alone, mates otherwhere,
Laughs more the closer clings Despair
To gnaw upon her heart. So fled
Her peace, and all the comely red
Of her fresh bloom began to fade.
She went at random, disarray'd,
A slattern in that trim-girt band
Of Hymnia's nuns who take their stand
Before their Saint, robed green and white
As hedgerows are in May, and bright
As hunter's horn their voices raise
The Chant Royal of Hymnia's praise.
Not now this company she dared
To lead, who once Choragus fared,
But slunk in last with hanging head,
Hoping to pass unvisited
Of that whip open eyes can wield.

Not thus she found her shame a shield
Nor sloth a buckler. Came a day
By Ladon's banks when morn was grey,
And the Sun's path not yet begun
Over the swooning hills. Cried one,
Plucking another, 'Ah, look there!
'Callisto's pinn'd her smock : a tear
'Below her girdle, and a stain—!'
Ah, slave of Love's, you pout in vain,
In vain grow hot! The chorus swells
Higher the more she storms, as bells
That peal together, clashing down
The din and hubbub of the town
On market days. Now Hymnia's come,
And sees her dear Callisto glum,
With cheeks all blubber'd, stormy lip,
And mutinous hands. For fellowship
She runs to shield, but is withstood
By the high duties of her blood
That may not touch what can defile,
Be't spotted robe or heart of guile.
She that loves Earth sees not earth-taint,
But goeth Innocency's Saint;
And being very Chastity
Maketh no choice what she shall be,
Nor findeth any sin a lure,
Since she sees nought but what is pure;
But slays the foul by one blank look
From her grey eyes. Callisto shook
To feel her now with untaught gaze
Send arrowing thro' her those cold rays

Steept in the Moon's bleak splendours when
She burns at full and maddens men
Drowsing beneath. She turn'd her face,
And blindly running fled the place
Where all her safety lay and pride,
Towards the great woods, there to hide
Among the tangled grass and fern,
And nurse her wound, and turn and turn
This side and that for a little ease
From aching.

There between the trees
The prying Fauns and Woodmen dark
And prick-ear'd Satyrs her did mark,
How all abandon'd to her mood
Of careless lovely lassitude—
So ripe, so melting, like a rose
That dewy-hearted throbs and blows
Languorous in the wind's caresses—
She lay becurtained in loose tresses,
Not seeing what her half-dropt zone
Let of her bosom's bower be shown,
Or that soft thing abeating there,
Ungirdled treasure, warm and bare.
And as they peept and spied upon
The goodly sight she made, came One
Adventurous, whom the Woodfolk dreaded,
Great Pan the goat-foot, horny-headed,
And saw her, and began to woo her
With his fierce music to undo her,
And make her former shames go pale
Beside her latter. Here's no tale

Leto's Child

For me who walk in Hymnia's beam,
Under her moon-wove eyes adream,
To tell you how Pan workt his will,
Or how she fended, with what skill
Garner'd within that sweeter nest
When she had laid on her Mate's breast,
And one the other comforted.
Little enough that serv'd her stead
This turn! Callisto was too tender
For the chill part: she must surrender.
Like white dawns hung in golden mist
That soon repent their wintry tryst
And go aweeping, she too soon
Gave him his hire, her body's boon;
And, all the kinder for late frost,
Was painful that he nothing lost
By tardy chaffering. So he brought her
To his tree-haunts, and lightly taught her
All of love's mystery; and this maid
For love's sake thought that well betray'd
Which had been life, had she but known it
As afterwards she had to own it.
    Ah, passion of the love-denied
    That ventures all for't far and wide,
    That lacking sweet love falls to foul,
    And feeds the flesh and starves the soul!
Her woe was working in her womb
Where that seed lay that was her doom:
Gotten by Pan, by Pan let lie
While he to other game gave eye,
Forgetful of what he had wrought

In the green forest when he taught
Callisto love, and found her apt.

Yet once again came Love and tapt
At her heart's gate in the soft guise
Of a young child, and her tired eyes
(Forsworn, forsaken !) lit from his,
And all her pent-up passionateness
Emptied upon him. Now she felt
The meed of sacrifice, who spilt
Her bounties there where she won more :
For mothers win who waste their store,
And for such gain a maiden lends
Herself, and garners what she spends.

Thus fared Callisto, Love's hot priest,
Kissing, who hoped not to be kist,
And loving askt but leave to love
Of that she courted. As he throve
Who now sat throned in heart and mind,
So she who gave herself all blind
To what came as to what had gone,
Deep in the woods where no sun shone
Nor any bird gave heartful note
(Save him who must, to slake his throat,
Love's hidden rhapsodist) ; where grass
Grew not, nor foot of man could pass—
Hid in the brake she made her nest,
And croon'd her song, and gave her breast
And all her fierce half-human soul

Unto that hour of joy she stole.
And who shall tell the raptures dim,
The strife to see, the rage, that slim
And pard-like creature passion'd there
With soul so dark in form so fair!
Only the hunger mothers have
Makes the wild gentle, cowards brave,
And shapes all women in one mould.

Now when Arcas was three years old—
For so she named him—Pan come thro'
The chestnut woods when a wind blew
Strong from the South, and bent all tops
Of trees one way, and heavy drops
Of rain drove pattering thick and fast;
And found the harbourage where had past
Callisto those three years of joy;
And found not her, but found the boy
At play with leaves the wind did lift;
And wonder'd, seeing how lithe and swift
He was, how bold to peer at him
Who watcht him there, shag-brow'd and grim,
With folded arms—old rugged Pan.
For as a mouse whom never man
Hath frighted, Arcas nosed and pried
Upon him curiously, and tried
To climb him, clasping in the pelt
Of his gross knees: which when Pan felt,
The God, whose storm of love or hate
Runs furious as an autumn spate
On foamy streams, his parentage

Of this bold minion leapt full rage,
And burn'd the sockets of his eyes
With smart of unused sympathies ;
And what he had seem'd light of worth
To what he had not since this birth
Hid in the green wood. Down he stoopt
And lifted up within his loopt
Engirthing hairy arms the child
Callisto bore him. Arcas smiled
And cheer'd to find himself so warm,
So snug enfolded out of harm.
And Pan began to sport and toy,
Bending his great bulk to the boy ;
Kist him full often, let him tweak
His knotty beard, and slap his cheek ;
Carried him pick-back, and at last
With him deep in the woodland past.

Picture who will the hot-foot leap
Of fear in her ; let who will weep
Her beggary, see her face drawn tight,
Her rigid eyes staring all night,
Too hard for tears ! Who has been mother
And lost her only child ? No other
Could read Callisto's anguish robb'd !
That grief is worst which is not sobb'd,
Nor thaw'd in tears ; and such was hers
Whose God was Arcas, and her pray'rs
Murmurs of happiness in him.
Poor atheist now, she faced the grim
Immense of dark as, in his cage,

Leto's Child

A gyved gerfalcon mews his rage,
Having a pain too deep for stress,
And thought too dim to voice duress.
Like some grey lonely rock at sea
Frayed by the waves' quiet onset, she
Who knew not how to weep nor die
Sat handfasted and felt the dry
Dull knife of Sorrow gride and grope
(Carving blunt-edged her horoscope),
And her heart's throb against her side,
While the vast night lay black and wide.
      But towards dawn, before the light
Was grey about her, down the night
Crept secretly a little breeze
Faintly and far, and brusht the trees ;
And here and there some quicken'd bird
Or shy terre-tenant cheept and stirr'd.
Then thro' the lattice of the leaves
She lifts her empty eyes, and heaves
One moaning sigh : then feels her tears.

As when a long frost breaks the weirs
And sluices serve but swell the flood,
So they and all that they withstood
Break bounds, and stream one leaping water,
So was Callisto, when Grief caught her,
Emptied in Grief's lachrymat'ries
Upon the salt wells from her eyes.
It seem'd the snows of all past years
Melted in them and gusht in tears,
And left her with a swept new heart,

A clean new sight of her old part ;
And eddied back those far-off days
She past with Hymnia on hill-ways,
When all the tired autumnal air
Trembled with morning blue and rare.
Still thro' the trees she saw how slept
The wide unruffled mere, and kept
Its silver silence. And the thought
How She in pity had ever brought
To mothers plenty for their lack,
Like tidal water stirr'd the slack
Of her dull blood unto the verge,
And floated her where Hope did surge.
Stumbling she rose up to her feet :
'I will go forth,' she said, 'to meet
'In her hill-precinct Artemis.
'It may be she will let me kiss
'Her loopéd vesture's hem, anoint
'Her feet with tears ; or she may point
'What way redemption might be sued.
'Ah, welcome She, whate'er her mood !
'Whether she stand up idly fair,
'Wreathing proud arms about her hair ;
'Or scornful be the silver line
'Burnt by her profile 'gainst the pine
'And laurel shade. Even if she grow
'Superb, and raise her height to bow,
'Or yet more barb'd than any dart
'Her eye-light flames, I will not start
'Nor cower nor cry out more than this—
'Pity all mothers, Artemis !'

Leto's Child

With that, all clothed and warm with love
As in a golden cloak, she drove
Her shames from off her ; keen and fleet
She wing'd the way with flying feet
That scarce shook dew from stalks of grass.
Over the high hills she did pass
As a white squall descried at sea
By ships becalm'd, that hug the lee
Creeping to windward ; nor slow'd pace
Nor slackt the tension of her face
Till she saw Menelaïs' shade
And what snug sanctuary he made
For Hymnia, on her fleece of wool
Calm-breathing, white and wonderful,
With her pure cheeks kist by her hair,
And her hands claspt.
On tiptoe there
Guilt-sore Callisto heard the beat
Of her prest heart fill that retreat
With riot. Long she cower'd prone,
As pilgrims creep before a throne
So holy that, unpurged by pray'r
And rite, they may not see it. There
Bowing she felt again the flood
Of her old pleasures throng her blood :
She sank on knees and quaking crept
Into the fleece where Hymnia slept,
And lay beside her, and clung and wept.
Then as warm tears fell on her cheek,
Whispering fast she 'gan to speak
(As if to have done ere she could wake)—

'White Virgin of the hill and brake,
'Mistress and Sister, Holy One,
'By thy pure face, by thy pure zone,
'By all my pains and forfeit bliss,
'Mother thou mothers, Artemis!
'Yea, tho' not love of Maid or Youth
'Ripen thy breast or draw thy mouth
'To need another's mouth or breast,
'And tho' not thou mayst feel the blest
'Estate we have—show all such grace!'
So pled she of the burning face.

Ah, guilty heart and guilty mouth,
Prodigal of thy blood and youth!
In vain to crouch for warmth and bliss
On the hid bosom of Artemis;
Between her arms look not to slip
To lie lockt there in fellowship:
That which burnt thee shall make Her cold,
That which thou bringst She cannot hold;
White lilies mate not roses red,
Nor snow with wine may mix and wed.
Lo now, she wakes: in her wet eyes
Shineth her joy, and with surprise
Struggles, and with dismay contends.
Or is sleep heavy still? Have friends
Gladness no more to find and knit
Each other? Or how cometh it
As one acquaint with grief she peers
Upon thee thro' a mist of tears?
Not glowing thro' them, as the sun

Beameth thro' fog ; but as they run
Freeing her sweet lids when they quiver
To bear their freight, the silver river
Wells up with tears to overbrim
The tender sluices. Now in dim
And hopeless sorrow she looks thee thro',
Held at arm's length, her pucker'd brow
Spelling her woe—Is this thy cheek,
This soiléd flesh ? What bruis'd lips speak ?
What message hath this rumpled frock,
What secrets can this belt unlock ?
Or when she leans to kiss and take
In arms this waif for old joy's sake :
'Alas, my mate and sister once,
'How art thou moil'd,' she cried, 'by chance
'To seem this stranger drugg'd with wine
'And feasting come to arms of mine ?
'Alas, I know thee not ! Thou art
'Like unto one who knew my heart,
'And my heart knew. Yet thou art not
'She : thou art sear'd, thou hast a blot
'Upon thee, making horrible !'
Nor would she suffer her to tell
Aught of her story, but still cried
As one in pain, and made to hide
Her face within her reedy gown.
  But then Callisto, passion-blown,
Stood up before her, and wail'd and said :
'Ah, would to God I had been dead
'Of any more cruel death than this
'That thou must deal me, Artemis !

'I am that wreckt Callisto, late
'A maid of thine, with thee. Ill fate
'Caused dark to fall where first was light,
'And smircht the robe thou gavest me white.
'Strike, therefore, Queen of hasty death!
'Let day break!' Hymnia held her breath
Ere she could draw it. Chill'd and sharp
Her young breath came. Then as a harp
Vibrating throbs sometimes and low,
She spake: 'Thou must die, but not now,
'Nor yet by me; for all that love
'I gave thee, and the scent thereof,
'Are still too sweet and fresh; the air
'Still breathes about my head that pray'r
'My mother made and still makes. Far
'Cometh its murmurous questing war
'From her high place, where she is set
'By Zeus,—lest haply I forget!
'Yet, having sinn'd, think not escape
'Awaits thee; thou shalt change thy shape
'From that thou hast, too far above thee,
'To that thou art. Oh, I did love thee!
'And still love my lost sister. Go!
'Thou art not she, who art soilèd so.'
Then on her fleece Maid Hymnia flung
Herself and wept. She was too young
For her high honour, and still gazed
Wistfully sometimes how she was raised
Alone, with all her tremors on her.
She was too young for her high honour,
Therefore she cried so bitterly.

But she that wrought this misery
Crept guilty forth to meet her fate
With the blunt paws and shuffling gait,
The mumbling motions of a bear.
Covered she was in pelt of hair,
Ruddy and rusty, shagg'd and coarse :
Gone her smooth treble, now a hoarse
And moody roaring serv'd her stead ;
Now she went dull'd, with blundering head,
Half blind with rage and thirst and lust,
To seek her meat ; and mad with dust
Stirr'd by her own gross haste. See here
The end of that hot charioteer
Who gives the loose rein to that horse
That needeth most the bridle's force !
Nor boots to tell how Arcas grew
Mighty hunter, or how he slew
Unknowing his mother ; nor how She
That loved her still raised her to be
A starry wreath when Heaven lies clear :
So in the sky men watch the Bear
Mount with the shining host, and tell
What was Callisto ere she fell.
  And thus sink they who serve Beauty
Otherwise than on bending knee,
Or dare to quench their fleshly dreams
At holy wells, in holy streams
To bathe their bodies. Beauty is rare
And delicate withal, so fair,
So thin a fabric, 'tis a breath
Of God's, whose prisoning is death.

Ah, my pale Hymnia, clear of brow,
Most holy and most shining! Thou
That o'er my waste of feverish days
Beaconest the lonely road with rays
Dipt in the moon. If aught in this
I dealt against thee, Artemis,
That all too eager and too rough
I sought and never had enough,
And lookt for what thou couldst not give me—
Turn pity on my head and shrive me.
Think of that height whereon we stood,
We alone, sphered in solitude,
And each the other's heart-hold eyed,
Till soul took wing to soul and cried.
So by that fire I took from thee
Then, and yet burn in, let me be
Not far away, that, even in prison,
I may watch thee, as in a vision,
Snow-white on some peak blue and cold,
Moon-toucht, and see thy rapt soul hold
Communion; see thee, from my bars,
Drink, motionless, the eternal stars!

THE NIOBIDS

Of windier days the havoc, in a song
More tragically swift; requited wrong
Wrought hastily by arrows, whose shrill hiss
Whistled a God's white passion, my tale is;
How Leto's children for their Mother spurn'd
Sought dreadful price, and how their anger burn'd
Unquenchable as new fire lightly leaping
About dry wood; of Niobe a-weeping;
Of flame from Heaven, of pity and young death,
Of grief too dry—tell now with sobbing breath.

Cut a thin reed from scream-beset Scamander
For hazard of this music! Let it wander
In outbursts harsh and crying as that moan
Heard in pent whispers—'Tower'd Troy is down!'
That so the passioning of that old pain
Quarried awhile in Thebæ come again;
So that old ghost evoke new founts of tears
From marbled Niobe, and on new ears
Her cry for pity fall. Make this thy chant.

Then sear the mouthpiece in a flame, and vaunt
Terrible Artemis, of curl'd-back lips,
And how her girdled bosom heaves and dips;
Sing of Cithæron shrieking, sing the scars
Not heal'd-up yet; picture what Arctic stars

That freeze, and burn in freezing, are her eyes ;
But seek not pity where it never lies
Contending ruthless Beauty and unkind.—
As well seek for it from the winter wind,
Boreas in his hollow-roaring caves,
Or from the storm-swept rocks beneath the waves
That headlong race over the ruinous white
Of beaten water : in these she hath delight
Where men go blencht and trembling ; ask not her
For courteousness who is no courtier.
Kneel to her when she fleets across the waste
Intent on killing, mindful she is chaste
Because no love she hath, but loveliness,
And because Beauty is its own mistress,
Is in itself its own accomplishment,
And of itself enamour'd and content.

In the green Age ere yet 'twixt Gods and men
That ill wind stirr'd that swept them out of ken
Each of the other, but God still paced his earth
And found it good, and men measured their worth
By his, yet went not utterly abased
To hide from him (as now) dumb and shamefaced,
Seeing him set so high ; in that green Age
When Zeus first massed his armaments to wage
Thunderous war upon the Titans' fame,
The hierarchs of hoar Olympus came
Unto their own : Zeus with his clanging crown,
Imperial Hera, Demeter looking down
Unto her mother-breasts (for ever full
Tho' drain'd for ever) ; Hestia with her stool

Set by the hearth and never to be moved,
And lame Hephæstus with that Bride he loved
And all must love who see, spite of the woe
She worketh, Aphrodite, with her slow
Long smile ; and crimson Ares whom Gods hate,
And only men serve blind and desperate :
These first ; and after them assuring peace
To who ensued it, came their sweet increase :
The calm delight and steady given in dreams
By her that wears the Ægis, on the beams
Of her grey orbs ; the blithesomeness and quick
Light glimmering of Hermes in the thick
And hive of marts and quays. Such grace was given
To man ; but Earth knew yet no Child of Heaven.
There only goatfoot elemental Pan
Held to the rule he had since time began ;
Nor had the ruddy stranger, Bacchus, yet
Brought ecstasy and torment and regret
To those who drank, and loathed, but drank again
His food of fire. But now at last the pain
Meek Leto suffer'd eased and sank in birth,
And a twin Godhead flusht the springs of Earth,
As I have told, unsacred, not revered,
Not shunn'd by men, nor sought ; not loved, nor fear'd.
In tender flesh hid-up of girl and boy,
This double Godhead (budding still and coy)
Lay nascent as the bloom upon a peach
Slow purpling to the Sun ; and each to each
In perfect tune grew shoulder unto shoulder,
Perfect in like and difference : she was colder,
Keener withal, in shape a maiden boy

By him, a boyish maid. She took her joy
Lonely upon the fir-clad hills, in woods,
In buffetting of winds, on river floods,
With beasts in covert and the hot-foot chase:
So her fierce pleasures tinted her fierce face
And hid her maiden softness out of mind.
He, with his yellow tresses unconfined
And his rapt look of meditative sight,
More as a maid was prone to red and white
That surged and follow'd hasty on his blood
As his thought pulst; so veil'd he in a hood
The God, as knights play palmer for a reason,
Veiling their strength. These waited their due season,
As hath been sung—he hid on Helicon
With his nine Witnesses, and she to run
On Mænalus' hoar summits, or the steep
Cyllené hath too rugged for the sheep:
With their own kind, the Dryads wild and shy,
These couchéd their immortal limbs thereby,
Unknown till Thebes wrought their Epiphany.

Amphion's wiſe, deep-girdled Niobe—
That same he brought from Phrygia and set up
To be a queen in Thebes and crowning-cup
Of bounties to the people, and to him
His bounty's well—when she, a maiden slim,
Suffer'd his yoke and bondage, on she took
Smooth matron's ways and dalliance forsook
With gossip-girls in girls' shy eagerness
To wonder at men's deeds; and with the dress
Of wife attuned her heart in graver mood

To bear the sober fruits of Motherhood.
A many children him in time she bore,
So many treasure-houses for her store
Of love which ever waxt as each new voice
Wailing for succour made her heart rejoice
That she was almoner. And even thus
Were her son's names :—Agenor, Phædimus,
Tantalus, Damasichthon, Ismenus, tall
Minytos, Sipylus ; and thus they call
Her daughters :—Chloris, Phthia, Ethodæa,
Astyoche, Ogygia, Asticratœa,
And white Cleodoche. Seven and seven
The gifts she won from God and made her heaven ;
And seven the shapely heads she lookt to crest
With war-gear, seven the stayers in the nest
Until that full time was for them to pair
And make her harbours many. She saw them fair
With her sweet favours, tall and keen and straight
As upland firs : unashamed in the gate
Amphion faced his foes, if foes he had,
Arm'd with his seven striplings prompt and glad,
Eye-tuned and lip-tuned unto all his will.
And she within the house, virginal still
In youth unending wrought by her snug ease,
Workt with her maiden witnesses : her knees
One claspt and knelt ; upon her lap lay one
Warm nestling ; Chloris, under her pure zone
Hugging her dream of spousals, loiter'd near,
Leaning upon her, whispering in her ear
Of all her pride and wonder to be wooed.
So prettily they chatter'd, as a brood

Of fledgelings cheep and preen and ape their mother,
While she in lazy bliss one and another
Watches and loves.
But when the long day drows'd
And fell asleep, and all the men were hous'd,
And Thebæ's streets were still—only the watch
Paced slow the ways looking at every latch
And eyeing every hurrier—she and they
Within the close-shut doors, in white array,
Gather'd to rid the Master of his toil,
Him and his sons, with unguent and sweet oil,
Washing of feet : all service of the house
They did, and comely serv'd the decent use
Of those old days, which saw woman most fair
When most man's helpmeet, and most debonair
When meekest. After this they sat at meat
In order due, and when desire to eat
And drink was put away, one with a harp
Would draw sweet verse from children's voices sharp,
And eagerly about that rafter'd hall
The anthem soar'd ; and lads and maidens all
Together singing made strong harmony
(Even as they lived harmonious). Only she,
Niobe, sat quite still and thrill'd apart,
Brooding upon her joy, and heard her heart
Follow the descant with its own strong rumour.

But, because stored love breedeth arrogant humour
In hearts that never can have love enough
For their own needs, and meteth measure rough
To hearts that go an-hunger'd (since they judge

All lack by their own joy), she bore a grudge
Against all women not in case like hers
Of splendid harvest, call'd them usurers
Who dared not spend the fat years lest the lean
Should come, and they be many who might have been
But two or three to fend for. Here her scorn
Cut like a whip: 'Better not to be born,'
(Cried she), 'than cumber earth with empty hives.
'We stub up fruitless trees; your barren wives,
'Your sleekbackt sepulchres, go quit, forsooth!'
Here she (the well of love) froze hard, sans ruth
Or pity: 'Let the sensual herd go dry!'
So she ran on, railing and bitterly,
But to her own clave close, and hour by hour
Spent of herself to feed them. All the flower
That breath'd from her she bent upon them, winning
New light from their light, strength from their beginning
To put strength on. So their tide flusht her tide,
And, as they grew in favour, she in pride.
Amphion, that old Minstrel, knew not Zeus
Or all his meinie; still the ancient use
Of Kronos and of Rhea, he and his house
Kept faithfully; for going prosperous
In the old ways men take them for a mark
And dread to swerve aside into the dark
Of new adventure: as in the tidal way
Above the weedy ooze stand bleacht and grey
The channel-posts, and point the cottage door,
The bleachéd nets and children on the shore,
So are the ancient Gods and the hoar rites
Men pay them still. But over Thebæ came

Blown on a dawn wind tidings of the fame
Of new unearthly visitants, of white
Clear forms seen sharply in the naked light
Before day broke—thunderous dawns, a flare
Across the still blue, flames driven thro' the air
From peak to peak, voices afar yet loud,
A great Shape stooping in a luminous cloud
Earthways, whereto the trees bent down their heads.
Men told of Hera, gracious to the beds
Of lowly Mothers when their pains began,
And how the cornheaps grew under the fan
When a grave Lady veil'd and gown'd in blue
Stretcht out her hands upon it. Chloris knew
(And whisper'd) how that night she must be wedded;
One came in rosy mist, a golden-headed
And supple laughing woman with a belt
Studded with beamy jewels, which when she felt
Clip her beneath her breasts, new long desire
She felt unto her lord, and a soft fire
Kindled the eyes of her and tinged her neck
So that unto his mind there was no fleck
Nor flaw in her young perfectness.
These things
Bruited about the Theban land on wings
Of rumour and low whisper, gather'd mass
With each new dawn; yet Niobe was crass
To whisper or low rumour: use and wont
Best fill'd her mind, she suffer'd no affront
To Cybele because Demeter went
Staidly among the corn beneficent;
Nor would know Zeus (tho' she had cause to know him

Who thrust her father Tantalus below him
Unto the misty realm of Hades, there
To choke with thirst, who once had drink to spare).
So when the news came shrilling like a horn
Thro' woodland hollows—Artemis is born!
And in the sky a sickle-moon, blood-bright,
Hung low above Cithæron all one night,
She neither heard nor saw, nor would. And when
After that moon had waned, unto all men
Next day-dawn came the news in murmurs hollow
As of wolves grieving—Born is great Apollo!
And then one long far cry—O Leto's glory!
Glory of Zeus! she scofft and made the story
A mockery for mothers—'Thus the hen
'Cackles (cried she), but not mothers of men.
'These lock their glory in the inner room
'Where their lords lie.' She turn'd unto the loom
And no more converse would she hold thereof.
　　But yet again she broke out into scoff
When one came homing breathless from the ships
With news of portents babbling on his lips;
How as he held his course on milk-smooth seas,
Standing for home, the holy Cyclades
Were throng'd with maidens, white-robed, wing'd and tall,
With hair like reedy gold, who one and all
Stretcht out their arms to Delos, and so stood
Motionless, prest for flight, in multitude
More wildering than snow-flakes, or those flocks
Of white sea-fowl that hive upon the rocks
Of ghostly Leuké (where the Heroes are);
Whom as he watcht, and trembled from afar,

A voice came wandering, like the long sea-cry
Of Glaucus thro' the dusk when fogs are nigh,
And air grew thick with wings, as all that crowd
Of glorious witness lifted as one cloud
Shining against the Sun, and lit and stay'd
On Delian Cynthos. Then he grew afraid,
And all his men afraid, and with the force
That comes of fear they wrested the ship's course,
And making Sunium, found the Eubœan bluffs
With a smooth channel, and no more rebuffs.
This was the tale he told to Niobe.
  There in the hall she reared her dignity,
Whenas by two her daughters she reclined,
And stared him silent. But deep in her mind
The thought bit acridly, and prickt her scorn
For Leto and her twins, the Delian-born
In whom all Earth was glad. It had been well
To know them God without that miracle
Which blared their truth and terror in one breath:
Yet who can watch for Fate or foreknow Death?

  In seven-gated Thebes the kingly seat
Over Ismenus sentinels, and it
Cithæron watches, peak on silent peak
Bathing in azure sky their summits bleak
And brown; but by the house, the riverside,
A marble terrace goeth, very wide,
Set orderly with pillars, whereupon
Cadmus and all his line still live in stone—
Cadmus who sow'd the seed and harvested
The Dragon's grain, and sweet Harmonia wed,

Whence grew a surer graft, that stately pine
Whose top was Œdipus, whose fall his crime.
Here on a day of heavy summer heat,
Under the leafy planes, whose branches meet
And knot and lace together there, the Queen
Sat gazing on the hills, across the green
Boeotian plain, over the forest deep
That lay aswooning till the noonday sleep
Of seaméd Pan were done; for while that holds
No shepherd boy dare venture up the wolds
To tell the sheep, nor breaketh any man
Upon that peace—so terrible is Pan!
  And as she sat came Phthia from the house,
Her youngest born, with blue eyes serious,
On tiptoe stepping, looking round in fear,
Who whisper'd, 'Hush, Maid Artemis is near!
'For up Cithæron with a flying throng
'Of nymphs and dogs I saw her go, and long
'I watcht as by they went, whirling as swift
'As forest leaves the North wind sets adrift.
'But one there topt the others by a head
'And seemed rather to glide, so smoothly sped
'Her naked feet, and so still was her way.'
Then Niobe—'Shall there never be stay
'Of talk of Leto and her boy and girl?
'Is it so wonderful a thing? O pearl
'Of mothers, whom I match with seven and seven!
'Could she no more, or tired the Lord of Heaven?
'Better look down to Earth for love and life:
'Yet Zeus's offcast who would take to wife?'

Ah, desperate words to launch, and overbold,
That reckon'd not who caught her word as told,
And lightly snatching it as lightly flew?
Echo! whose hiding-place is in the blue
Dim wrappage of the valleys, where she lurks
Cooling her breast against the hills, and irks
Only at silence, for she feeds on noises
Of tumbling rocks and brooks, and men's clear voices
Raised on the uplands to call home the sheep—
Echo caught up that word and 'gan to leap
And toy with it, as children toss the leaves
To watch the wind whirl them above the eaves;
Or as that same wind spires the sand she did
With Niobe's defiance; so it slid
On the swift stream o' the wind, and Echo flasht
Silverly after it, caught it, and dasht
Into the current's core with it, and carried
It up towards the hill-top, where now tarried
Young Artemis, bathing her ardent face
In the wind's wave, come newly from the chase.
Thrown backward was her head upon her hands,
Her throat lay bare, but yet the jealous bands
Guarded her bosom crosswise: thus she lean'd
Deep breathing, while about her the air keen'd
Shrilly, and whistling on it Niobe's word
Struck at her cheek. She quiver'd. As a bird
Putteth his head askance and sideways peereth
To watch that way where the stirr'd brush he heareth,
And seems to hear with eyes, so quick and tense
Look they about—so she with every sense

Heard this—'With Leto I match seven and seven!
'Could she no more, or tired the Lord of Heaven?
'Better look down to Earth for love and life:
'Yet Zeus's offcast who would choose?'
The strife
That caused her press her heart did sweep and surge
Across her face, as clouds drive up and scourge
The golden hillsides, changing all to dun
And dreariment that mellow'd in the Sun.
Her eyes were frozen lakes, whose sullen glass
Gave out no hint of how the child did pass
Before the dawning God not yet discern'd:
All the red blood she had blazed up and burn'd;
It seemed her slender body scarcely stay'd
The throbbing of each pulse of fire, but sway'd
And flickered as the gauzy filament
That wraps the lantern flame. But it died spent
Palely before her purpose gaining grip
That held the blood still in her bitten lip,
And in her clencht-up hands, whose little palms
Bore the cruel imprint of her nails. So calms
Her sobbing side, so hard and frosty light
Glitters within her eyes; and she takes flight
Sheer down the stony reaches of the hill,
Trailing a flame-bright wake. Ev'n as to kill
Stoops the grey osprey to the sea, as stoops
The white sea eagle, as the gannet droops
His wings and tumbles headlong on his prey,
So the Death-Maiden on her shrill foray
Flew; and in peaceful valleys and still woods
Darkling below her hid the timid broods

Of deer and cattle, fearing that blind storm
The North wind drives; the hare croucht in her form,
Lest this were eaglet sweeping woodsides bare
Of those shy things that leap and nibble there.
Heedless of them she wings above the brake,
Over the open moorlands, by the lake
Solemn and deep in shade: the white-faced coots
Huddle together, watching where she shoots
Starlike across the pool of cold green sky
That mirrors them and is their canopy
And utmost dream. But when the sable dark
Fell, she flew lower, as above the park
The white owl softly courses; as he cries
His long lone cry, so she, and swept her eyes
Free of her clinging hair, and tiptoe stood
Peering upon the black edge of a wood
Where the dim sides ran back between the stems
And shelving branches of the firs.
(In dreams
Oft have I been there with her, mystic, dark,
With sombre eyes and finger warning—'Hark!
'Listen and watch; you have all that you pray:
'Divine my heart-beats, read the thing they say.
'See now, I tremble!' Her cheeks and pale mute lips
Come near—I look, and hear above the drips
Of winter rain her heart's quick answers fall,
Speaking her soul!)
Out of the wood a call
Borne on a little sighing wind came far,
Voicing again her urgency: a star
Fitful and low went wandering out and in

The velvet dark, and all the tree-tops thin
Seem'd beaten by a sudden breeze, and bent
Their plumy heads. And as it came and went
It grew apace until it steept the night
As with shed effluence from a veiléd light
Diffuse and glowing. Nearer and more near
The wood's recesses open'd, sharp and clear
The little tree-trunks stood, and every blade
Of grass and each fern tendril cast a shade
Of pitchy night. But down the tunnel'd flare,
Lovely, with fire-fraught eyes and blown-back hair,
Loxian Apollo flew to Artemis
And call'd her by her name.

Softly did kiss
The twin-Gods, hand in hand, one to the other
Leaning till their cheeks toucht ; then to her brother
Maid Artemis her passion-wounded side
Easéd of what within did throb and chide
In broken accents : sobs and hinted tears
Clouded her stormy voice, wherein like spears
Of summer lightning leapt her wrath. Then low
And stilly as black water glides thro' snow,
She urged him to redeem as with a rod
Of steel that wrong done her who (loving God)
Was of God loved, and hid within her womb
Witness of high espousal. Thro' the gloom
And murk of that hot night her dreadful face
Of terror fraught with beauty told her case
More cryingly than her vibrating tone.
The girl's heart bled, the Goddess's was stone.

Apollo marks the tempest in her, heeds

Her chlamys billowing like a bed of reeds
Stir'd by the river's bosom when a storm
Blows from the South and the flood-water warm
Wells up insurgent. So she stood and shook
With both hands holding his. An arrowy look,
A high look as a lion's when he wakes,
Caught him from her and glinted. Quick he takes
His golden bow and bends it down, pulls home
The tense cord, breathing low, Come, sister, come!
Nor past between them any further word,
But each went lightly forward, undeterr'd
By pity such as wringeth men, or shiver
For apprehended death. No wink or quiver
Falter'd their solemn eyelids sternly set
Back from those eyes which tears could never wet
Nor joy make brighter. Side by side they rose,
And hand in hand went smoothly, even as flows
Some lordly river's volume to the sea
With scarce a ripple, and not hastily,
As lest their wrath might ebb or lose its spell.
But high as o'er the sea-fret and sea-swell
Lonely and questing sails the albatross
Thro' dim blue leagues no other life may cross,
Not eager and not slow, with calm wing-sweeps—
So high, so rapt they oar'd the skyey deeps.
Nothing so steadfast nor so keen felt Earth
As she felt them, that sought with such still mirth
The harvest of their arrows: breast to breast,
Breathing together, over crest and crest
Of the sleep-folded mountains, plains of grass
And bending corn, o'er fog-enwrapt morass;

The Niobids

Where sandy reaches are, where the lagoon
Lies cold in sleep, death-stricken by the Moon ;
Thro' cloud and shatter'd mist that sweep the night
And mass in secret ; by the inner light
Of their own starry eyes they wing'd their way,
Till over Thebes they lit, and waited day.

Over against that city on the scarp,
Where it juts boldest to the sky with sharp
Tooth'd fret, the Theban kings had cut a ledge
Deep in the rock's heart, midway 'twixt the ridge
And plain below, where dream'd the marble town
Terraced above Ismenus, with its crown
Of temples to the elder Gods—Kronos,
Rhea and Gê, and murder'd Ouranos ;
And on that shelf mid-set from Earth to Heaven
The Queen with her seven sons and daughters seven
Made to Eileithyia daily dues
Of wheatflour cakes, and (from a golden cruse)
Sweet olive oil ; and daily when the rite
Was smoothly finisht, one upon the height
Soon as he saw the priest bow and retire
Kindled a beacon, and the sky caught fire,
And the Sun rose, and day began its round.
So did they ever.
Now that night profound
Roll'd back in mists, and washt the city bare,
And slowly lifted up the rock-hewn stair :
Higher it swept and higher, and as the lids
Of grey-eyed Morn flutter'd, the Niobids'
Muezzin-call to prayer from height to height

Shrill'd solemnly in that shadowless light;
And as it rang about the iron chain
Of watching mountains, slowly down the plain
Came Niobe, and slowly clomb the stair,
And after her her children, pair by pair,
White-robed, bare-headed, as for sacrifice
Sweeten'd and pure. Slowly towards the skies
They mounted by the winding way, and stood
Upon the ledge in meek fair attitude
Of folded hands and down-dropt eyes demure.
Ah, little flock! Ah, passion of the pure!
What have ye here to do, that cannot spy
What scarr'd Cithæron holds against the sky?

Day came in fire, red splinters spiked the East
Behind the mountain summits, and increast
Their awful shade, until the flood of Morning
Should overbrim their banks and set them burning.
Now hath the priest set out the altar, laid
The wood, the frankincense; the prayers are said
Whose lifting-up should be the column'd flame
From off the hill.

That day there never came
The leap of fire, nor ever more should dart
Fire from that precinct. For Phthia held her heart
And sobb'd and fell down; and her mother turn'd
Holding the torch aside, kneeling, and yearn'd
Over her while she counted her faint breaths
And saw creep up that colour which is Death's.
Was that sharp cry, half choking and half grief,
Agenor's? Lo, he smileth; but no leaf

Strung to the aspen by invisible thread
Shivers more lightly—nay, he droops his head
Into his bosom suddenly ! The rest
Is folding of the hands upon the breast.

Pity this woman's palsied tongue and eyes !
She cannot pray, nor tend her dead : no cries
Hath she to Gods for pity. Quick and fast
The unseen arrows fall. As snaps the mast
Under the roaring weather out at sea,
Ismenos bends his neck. Astyoche
Cover'd her marr'd fair face ; Chloris did pillow
Over her heart Ogygia for bedfellow
And slept with her : only a little frown
Ruffled her brow, as tho' the pain came down
Too suddenly to let Death's final peace
Float out the soul. But not such calm decease
Suffer'd the brothers ; but they fought the odds.
For Phædimus stood up fronting the Gods,
And bared his throat, and raised the Theban shout
Ere he fell breast-shot. Tantalus held out
His arms to shield Cleodoche, and faced
The storm enfolding her : the arrow laced
The two in one. So breast to breast they died,
Lovely in death and loving. Thro' her side
Asticratœa, slim and queenly, felt
The agony, so stumbled, crawl'd and knelt
Before the Queen, and bowing down her head
Unto her feet, slept then. But one had fled
Earlier to that poor mother, seeking there
Sanctuary, childlike, on her bosom bare ;

And strain'd herself to her—but suddenly
With two quick throbs constricted and lay still,
Dead weight: O Death, hast thou not yet thy fill?
So dropt they all, riddled by unseen death,
Secretly stung by pain that caught the breath
And leapt an entry. Like the flickering tongues
Of that blue wrath which unto Zeus belongs,
The sightless arrows curl'd and hist their way;
And so they died in all their fresh array
Of youth unprized, unknowing and not praying
Mercy or piteousness, and never saying
'Farewell!' or 'Pray for me'; nor could they know
Above Cithæron who bent back the bow,
Or what slim Archers, glittering in the Sun
As cut in pillar'd ice, this work had done.
  But Niobe, when lonely she did stand
Among her dead, she knew! and stretcht her hand
Towards them for a stroke the more, one stroke
That had been merciful. But Phœbus spoke
Clear down the mountain's flank: 'O Niobe,
'Ill didst thou do, and now hast ill for fee.
'Therefore beware of strife with God.' But she,
His sister swift, that never looketh back,
Spake nothing, but let go the bowstring slack,
And drew her girdle higher and more taut
About her bosom, looking on what she wrought
With level gaze unflinching. And the dawn
Fill'd all the plain with light from lawn to lawn;
And Artemis fled shrilling down the wind.

Still gazing stood that mother, stricken blind,

The Niobids

Rigid in grief that stony is and numb,
For that it biteth in and leaveth dumb
The lips, and sealeth up the fount of tears.
And still, men say, her lonely image rears
A marble head among the empty hills,
But now 'tis scored about with countless rills
Whereby the traveller, hearing all the waters,
Knows Niobe weeps yet her sons and daughters.
For, having pity on that grief so dry,
Our Lord Apollo gave her grace to cry :
Kinder than She (whose kindness were to kill),
The Mistress of the cold nights on the hill ;
Whose footfall is the soughing of the trees,
And her white splendour seen when moonbeams freeze
The bleacht earth huddled lowly on the plain ;
Who slays and passes, looking not again ;
Who, all too lovely to be loved, still goes
Guarding with steadfast eyes her breast of snows.

LATMOS

PROEM

THE shepherd boy, whose russet beauties seen
By hazard of the Huntress Maid had been
A torch to kindle flame in her cold side
And prick a wound in that whole heart and clean,
Endymion, wrought in great verse, lives enskied :
Yet his adventure fell not thus I ween.

God made us men, and straight we men made God
No wonder if a tang of that same sod
Whereout we issued at a breath should cling
To all we fashion ! We can only plod
Lit by a shaveling candle, and we sing
Of what we can remember of the road.

Ah, Poet, whose clear taper, casting beam
Wider than England, made far Hellas gleam
Bright as the veins in hoar Pentelicus,
Or that hid mount where still the old Gods dream
In marble desolation ! Never thus
Hellas knew Hymnia of the wood and stream.

Ah, Hymnia, young shy haunter of the brake,
Breath of the North-West wind ! what black wood-lake,
What purple fell, what stretch of heath and down

That ever felt thy quick feet, would not take
Its parable up and bid the hill-wind drown
The singing voice that such false song could make?

Hymnia, the youngest Goddess, Leto's child,
The dauntless Virgin! She, the undefiled!
She, Lovely Wretch, leave fingering her dart,
And lean to hear the languid accents mild
Of calf-love, pressing one hand to her heart!
She, Guarded Lips, to kisses reconciled!

We give no crown where love may not be sped,
We think not sacrosanct a maidenhead;
We bid such seek their master in a man;
Woman we say's no woman till she wed.
But she that roams the woods is of such plan
No love could woo her to a bridal bed;

Being the very Form of straining Youth,
The sting and throb of young blood without ruth;
Passion that leaps before the senses wake,
Thorn'd Pudency, the petulance of truth;
Chastity going arm'd, yet quick to take
Cold pleasure or hot rage—or both, in sooth.

If you have seen her like, in yet-skimpt gown,
Roving at careless will, her bright hair down
Her shoulders—mark her well: she plays the boy,
Knows not of languor nor the airs of town,
The sighing nor the trembling: all her joy
Sparkles in her red lips and cheeks wind-blown.

Love her, yet see no word nor hint of it
Come near her. She is fierce, you may be bit.
Bitten you will be by your shameful thought
To dare a blush on that front all unwrit
With your stale learning. Too soon she'll be taught,
And ply you flash for flash of your thin wit.

Love is not all the art of life. Take joy
That God still deigns to leave us girl and boy ;
And still a pure breath issues clean and sweet
From lips unwelded in the dull alloy
We're stuck with. Let us pray to sanely eat
Life's cates, so their sharp savour may not cloy.

I.

On Latmos' side one drowsy summer night,
Full of soft influences, dark delight,
Lit fields of magic, chasms, ghostly trees
Windless and calm, beneath the patient sight
Of the full moon, Endymion stretcht at ease
Upon the sward, lay wondering at the light.

He was that half-ripe age when Love first flushes
The tingling blood with his insurgent rushes,
When reflex languors make the senses faint,
And heart-beats tell their tale in burning blushes ;
When the distress those crying signals paint
Hints homing foes in undescried ambushes.

To wit, within the mind those foemen lurk,
And there fermenting darkly do their work,
With phantasms for lures, and whims to cheat us,
Green-sickness for their hid and stabbing dirk,
And feverish nights for sticks wherewith to beat us
To luxury undream'd by any Turk.

Beardless he was and tender, yet he had
The nervy look of something swift and glad,
A mountain look of merlin or spar-hawk :
Strain'd sharp his lips were ; peasant-like yclad
In sheepskin and white linen, his light walk
On sprinting toes show'd him no peasant lad.

Below him as he lay the muffled sheep
Like tombs adown the hillside seemed to creep.
On that blue silence the far dog-wolf's bark
Came moaningly, as if one in his sleep
Mutter'd and turn'd round to watch out the dark :
The air was thick with moon-dust, golden, deep,

All the night tense for witchcraft. In clear sky
The white moon seem'd to burn ; her open eye
Laid spell upon him, that he heard the beat
Of his quick heart thrill expectation high—
If some shy Nymph with dim and naked feet
Should flit across the fell, and he be by !

Even as he wonder'd, on his reel'd sense came
In palpitant light a maiden, bright as flame
Beaten thin, high and eager, with great eyes

Whose long set look call'd stammering and shame
Upon him. Slim she was, of middle size ;
Too tall to plead, too slight his love to claim.

Her thin white raiment, loopt up high, reveal'd
Her thong-girt knees ; her bosom was conceal'd
By cords bound crosswise over it, as if
She trod the moors adventurously, steel'd
'Gainst what her beauty's bane was ; and as stiff
She held herself as flower-stalks frost-congeal'd.

And as she gazed, he gazed with eyes as wide,
With wonderment breath'd pantingly, and sigh'd
To deem a thing so delicately fair
Should visit him asleep—softly to glide
Down the long argent flights of the moon's stair,
Impalpable, in moonbeams steept and dyed.

She seem'd a thing compact of windy water
And rays of light, as if the Sun had wrought her
Of his own fire, and temper'd what he made
With the cold ripple whence his skill had caught her.
From him she had her beam of falchion-blade,
In all else of shrill wind she was the daughter.

She watcht him stilly, then upon her lip
Her finger lit and toucht, as if to clip
The flying word ere it had leapt her throat
To hail him ; yet a half-smile she let slip
The leash, and strung his heart to a bold note,
To ask the grace of her good fellowship.

Latmos

'O thou (he said) whose coming brings no ease
'For dread of thy quick going! if in peace
'Thou visitest alone these dreamy places,
'Stay now; the dawn stirs not yet in the trees,
'The night is high, the Waggoner still paces
'His starry road—ah, quieter than the breeze

'Of earliest morning when the first flush takes
'The outposts of the hills, and all wood-brakes
'Are quicken'd with bird-voices: art thou chill?
'Come, play with me: the night in my blood aches.
'Clear is thy gown for running: climb the hill,
'Or race me down, an oak-wreath for the stakes!'

She still lookt at him sideways, as a bird
Darkling in covert listens if he heard
A menace to his haven; still she kept
Her warning finger up; evenly stirr'd
Her raiment where her hidden bosom slept:
But now she chose to take him at his word.

Upon her parted lips and gleaming teeth
He saw frank pleasure hover like a wreath;
Her eyes danced unto his, and call'd—then swift
As a sword flashes outward from the sheath
She fled away over the stony drift
Of rugged Latmos, out upon the heath.

Nor was he slow to chase, so hither, thither,
This way and that they glinted close together;
She led him in deep fern where, thro' the thicket,

She wing'd on like a bird with unruff'd feather ;
Then out towards the plain, as a young pricket
That skips to feel the kiss of open weather.

She lookt not back ; he labour'd all he knew
To win her arch face to his sidelong view ;
The nimble blood ran crimson in her cheek,
Her wavy hair let loose and backward flew ;
He set his teeth, wasted no breath to speak.
The sheep lookt up and scatter'd from the two.

He battles languor stealing up his limbs,
He labours with his breath, his eyelight dims ;
Lightly she leads him thro' a birchen copse
Between whose silver shafts the moonlight swims
In plashy pools. She slackens speed and stops ;
Joy wells in her full eyes and overbrims.

There as she bent her head, he came and crown'd
With oak-leaves her bright hair ; and all around
Ambrosial fragrance lifted. Being so near
Her quicken'd breath fann'd on his cheeks ; the sound
Her knocking heart made thrall'd him—to be here
With her alone !—her willing slave and bound.

'O who art thou ? What moorland or what tree
'In forest ambush holds and harbours thee ?
'Teach me thy cunning—stay a little while !
'Leave me not yet, but where thou dwell'st bring me !'
She breath'd more quickly, with a shy slow smile :
Then, 'Come and see,' she said, and, 'Come and see.'

She led him (willing convoy) thro' a dell
Of feathery trees whereon the moon's deep spell
Sat brooding, and the hollows of the wood
Loom'd blue and cold. He follow'd, liking well
The glimpses of her face which thro' the hood
Of her untrammel'd hair his eyes could tell.

So they two went towards a mighty beech
Standing alone, whose shelving boughs did reach
Over thick fern and foxgloves ; where a rill
Made night melodious with its silver speech :
And there she stopt and listen'd, standing still,
Holding her lips—and each waited for each.

And thro' the trees the Dawn came up all red,
Blushing to be so new from Tithon's bed,
And dappled all the way with rosy flame ;
Which seeing she grew pale, and whispering said,
'Follow you back the road wherein you came :
'I may not bide with you '—and lightly fled.

II.

Ye charm'd haunts of the Wood-folk, shrill romance
Of cypress-glades wherethro' the Dryads dance !
O upland heather, where in misty heat
The brown hills swoon, and we watch in a trance
And think to hear them thud with the quick beat
Of linkéd Oreads footing white advance !

Ye have a spell on you, which whoso feels
Grows greater than his lot, sweet poison steals
Thro' all his veins ; and he, pale postulant
At first, stands up initiate, and reels
To learn the secret stir, the underchant
Of those dim spaces which the rite reveals.

But he who meets with Hymnia where she strays
With her heart bare upon the windy ways
(When she and the wild weather beat as one),
Hath draught of wine to madden all his days
With longing to drink deeper, nor to have done
Till all his force be lavisht in her praise.

Speak not of friendship as of man for maid ;
The thing is not nor can be. She's repaid
Her bosom-beats of welcome with a doubt
What such light prize be worth : if she is staid,
His forces mass to carry her redoubt.
No truce ! the man is master of his trade.

She slower puts off childhood, longer clings,
More wistful feels the throb of her new wings.
A Mother from her nurse-days, her warm breasts
Are ever milky ; one by one she brings
The stragglers home, serves motherhood's behests :
Answer'd by treachery, she hides the stings.

Endymion, all the Man in him alight,
Trackt thro' the day the passes of the night ;
And 'Here we greeted,' 'Here she lay a-hiding,'

'Twas now she flasht, a snow-bird in her flight';
And 'Here she paused in pity of my chiding,'
And 'Here she vanisht straightly from my sight!'

He markt the very trees where in her speeding
Her light caress had lit; he fell to reading
The turf to find the imprint of her feet:
He kist them hotly with a heart all bleeding,
All torn and macerate; yet found it sweet
To raw and probe the wound she set him feeding.

The hairy Satyr mumbling in his den,
The frolic Fauns, the Nymphs of fern and fen,
Hid up their twinkling eyes and stuff'd their mouths
With leaves to choke their merriment. O men,
O heroes so brain-valorous, O ye youths,
Befogg'd so quick by things beyond your ken!

They knew her! Every woodland elf must cower
And blink and slink before her cold bright power.
Whenas she with her maidens held the chase
Those goatfoots grumbled, but could only lower
Under the leaves: no male dared show his face
When Hymnia chose the greenwood for her bower.

Them reckt our hapless lover not, a clamour
Of trumpets burnt his mind; he could but stammer
Her name in broken syllables; his head
Throbb'd; on the silence tickt the incessant hammer
Of pulses fierce upon his brows. So sped
Day after day, and each heapt-up his glamour.

The nights fell, violet-lidded, dusted gold,
The hills were silent, silence wrapt the fold ;
And silence mockt him. Ribbon-like the road
Wound pale and stealthy over the dun wold.
No footfall echoed, vacant the moon show'd
Vacancy, skyward, earthward, large and cold.

Love feeds on penury, is Woe's belonging :
Still sterner grew his need, and still came thronging
Gleams of her shy pois'd head, her wayward fashion
And pretty petulance, the swift bright conning
Of all his soul her eyes took ; thus his passion
Foster'd his thought, and thought but nurst his longing.

He sought her ever while the long days dragg'd,
And long hot nights ; his ardour never flagg'd.
A parching fire consumed him, clinging thirst ;
He was beset, bewilder'd, mired and quagg'd :
He dared not give her up—he was accurst
In this, his body, not his spirit lagg'd.

Now when he falleth faint, and old Despair
Sits down beside him, with her grizzled hair
And mouthings vain and witless waving hands,
To ape his wretchedness—lo ! all the air
Thrills sentient awakening, and she stands
With frank blue-beaming eyes before him there ;

And breath'd again that music wrought in stone,
The carol of Messenic Damiphon,
Caught when the April woodland, dewy wet,

Stirs amorously to the new-risen Sun—
The bloomy transience of a violet,
The ripple of a brook, a wood-bird's tone !

A-trembling fell he that such radiant flesh
(He deem'd it), palpable and sweet and fresh,
Should stand so near in girlhood's laughing mien
Glimmering there. Two dogs she had in leash,
A quiver and long bow ; her bodice green
(So trim it was) drew closer his heart's mesh.

Her mood was tender. As in April veers
The vane, and drives the Sun to shine thro' tears,
She through her pleasure lookt, her shining eyes
Struck a warm wave of light upon his fears,
And his eyes fill'd with dimness. Thus one vies
The other's welcome, shy glance shy soul cheers.

At last, 'Oh, why are you so late ?' he cries,
And has her hand. She suffers, but soon tries
To disengage, shake off ; for strangely mingles
With her cool blood the fret whereof he dries
And wastes ; and strangely burns her cheek and tingles
With unus'd blushes, unguess'd fantasies.

Therefore she frees herself soon as she may,
With wooing whispers coaxes him to play
As that first night of meeting. He no whit
Laggard in what will keep her, says not nay ;
Yet feigns to halt, that longer he may sit
To dally with her sweet insistent way.

'Come up,' she cried, 'thou sluggard, wilt thou drowse
'While I stand pleading?' She bars her milky brows,
Stamps her bare foot, and plucks him by the smock
(He asks no better, rogue he is), unbows
Her budded lips to open, strains to evoke
Spirit like hers, untiring till he rouse.

Then with what pretty air of triumphing
She pull'd him to his feet, and bid him sing
His happiness at having newly found her;
Next, as a swallow slants on stiff-pois'd wing,
Ere he could ope his mouth, her skirts tuckt round her,
She skimm'd the hill, scarce brushing on the ling.

Unleasht, her yelping hounds held sinuous chase,
Endymion, on his mettle, made good pace;
The long night echoes woke the glens and hills,
The moon reel'd in the sky with a scared face
To see their revelry: but nothing skills
To warn the enamour'd wretch his anxious case.

Oh, boy bewitcht! O summer nights! Ah, gold
And glamour! Soon, too soon must come the cold:
The frost will come to blight your happy sport
And leave your years remember'd as tale told.
Think not to carry with you into port
Young treasure, all your days to have and hold!

But this there is to say, not everyone
Quaffs such full measure as Endymion;
For few there be so delicately blest

With sight of that fair Child that flies alone.
Yet every boy Love shines on, be it confest,
Is apt to take his candle for the Sun.

Alas ! he had been happy had he dwelt
Coequal with his mates, and never felt
The burning cold of that immortal vision
Wherein his heart must freeze as his love spilt :
Sheerer his fall the higher he was risen,
Madder his wreck the more she was misspelt.

Not far the end of him and all his pleasure,
For soon Fate measur'd him who set no measure
To hold his boundless needs or give him pause
Ere in his haste he had let slip his treasure
Into deep water. Yet now she sheathes her claws
And leaves him toying to await her leisure.

Who blameth Hymnia may go blame the wind
That battles thro' the trees and strews behind
A wreckage of torn branches, whirling leaves,
Reprove the leaping flood-tides, or the blind
Mad onset of the rain on cottage eaves :
Such things are lovely, not unkind nor kind.

So she, that darling voice of wind and weather,
And wayward wandering breath no man could tether,
Herself shook loose the reins and played at folly,
Not knowing what she wrought, nor recking whether
She wrought at all. Endymion's melancholy
Blacken'd his own joy and her joy together.

But many hours of joyance yet they had
Wherein to frolic artless lass and lad.
She stayed not, having found him to her taste ;
He school'd himself in her light to be glad :
Taught by her limpid candour he kept chaste
In mind. Yet groped that worm that drove him mad :

That vile worm Gluttony, that makes man lanker
The more they feed him, gnaw'd him on to hanker
More than she had to give ; she had no will
For more than simple pleasure, his was ranker
(Being mortal) : so he workt to have his fill
And cherisht secretly that old worm's canker.

III

O ye who have markt the Huntress in soft guise,
With Child writ candid on her mouth and eyes,
And stripling in her motions, have a heed—
She may be terrible, she takes reprise ;
Her Father's lightning ruins at her need,
Her eye-burn carries death on whom it flies.

Betrayed Callisto, ambusht in her lair,
In vain she thought to lurk ! The arrowy stare
Pierced thro' her pelt to see her what she was,
And death struck cold the girl's heart in the bear ;
Tityos, burly giant, stretcht his mass—
Nine leagues of bleeding flesh and torment there !

Orion, that great hunter! Chios knows
His end: no strength avail'd to meet such foes
As Hymnia wing'd upon him; but he past,
And still in Hell pursues with empty blows
Shadowy game in shadowy antres vast,
And still exults to watch their shadowy throes.

Now thus Endymion reapt the seed he cast her—
He could not mate with her, he must be master.
Seeing the girlish bloom she had, he claimed it
His due by right of manhood. Fast and faster
He bound himself. No matter what he named it
(Twas folly or fate), he brought his own disaster.

Desire to seize that which he loves, to hoard
His treasure and to keep it lockt and stored,
Makes man a usurer, who like a miser
Goes beggar'd, slave where his own flesh is lord—
Rebellious slave! Our youth, no whit the wiser,
Ached now to set a Goddess at his board.

As well build walls to cage the Wind o' the West,
Or try to curb the ocean billow's crest;
As well dam up the well-spring of the rains,
As look for Artemis, in stuff gown drest,
Go soberly about her household pains,
Meek household drudge, with babies at her breast!

Infatuate fool, he husbanded his skill
What time her innocency rompt its fill.
She more bewitcht him in that she was gay,

Seduced him most where least she thought of ill.
He suffer'd her to tease, it serv'd his way;
For thus he thought to trap her to his will.

Then came a night when long and far they stray'd,
Flying from golden light to purple shade;
And long and far their calling rent the night,
But yet he was no nearer what he pray'd;
For all so soon he near'd her she took flight,
And when she rested his heart grew afraid.

Slyly he then devised another race,
How she should lead a scarf and he should chase,
Seeking to win it from her by a snatch.
She with a laugh agrees and runs apace;
He follows stoutly—'tis a level match:
Whereso she twists the hound is on her trace.

Her hair flies back (he is not far behind)
And stings him to more speed; the amorous wind
Wraps his Belov'd and him in one caress.
She holds the prize aloft; he has no mind
To clutch it, being set on nothing less
Than her free hand in his to be confin'd.

Which now he has achiev'd; her hand in his
Lies still as a caught bird, so warm it is,
So breathing with her strife to win back breath:
He marketh her his prize; her tumbled dress,
The sweet disorder tremulous beneath,
Urge to new conquests, new captivities.

More than she hath to spare! even to taste
Her unapproachable lips, to belt her waist.
Think her not arch; no simulated ice
Crusting an inner fire show'd she. If chaste
She prov'd, 'twas not she tarried to be nice,
But all her body to her mind was braced.

For while she walkt his prisoner, held secure,
Other thought took her; dovelike and demure
She rested passive while her fancy ruled
The empyreal heights, enthron'd and pure,
A very Goddess—whom he thought to have school'd
With his man's wit his bondage to endure.

Holding to what he had (while bad was best),
He took no joy o't, coveting the rest;
Handlockt they stray'd, he trembling, she afar,
Quiring in thought, but never less possest
Than when he led her captive; her mind's car
Lifted her out of ken. She held her breast.

The couchéd flowers that lay embraced in bed
Made nuptial music to him as he led
Her to a thicket; yet scarce dared he lean
Nearer than touch her garment. She not stay'd
Him stick a rose-knot in her bodice green:
He thrill'd to touch her—yet no word he said.

He sat, and drew her down beside him; there
A little space they rested, while the air
Fann'd her hot cheeks and blew a flame to his;

Gentler she grew and yet more softly fair ;
And still her hand keeps harbour where it is,
And still he longs, but not enough to dare.

Even as a virgin to whom love is new
And wooing terribly sweet she was to view,
Her chin upon her hand, her eyes downcast ;
A meek smile flutter'd on her lips, withdrew,
Hover'd again : the roses flusht and past
Her neck and cheeks, then flooded her anew.

One little bare foot danced beneath her frock,
Her blowy hair went free ; a vagrant lock
Play'd truant from her snood and o'er her shoulder
Claspt at her neck. Her eyes that could be rock
And freeze the Gorgon stiff, now made him bolder,
So wistful soft they seem'd, so wide from mock.

What youth seeing Beauty in a melting mood,
Awaiting love, will stint his love its food !
Who in soft moonlight, secret with a maid,
Would stay to dam the torrent of his blood,
But rather would not urge it on to raid,
And crest himself triumphant on the flood ?

Ah, silly child, that could not be contented ;
Ah, lovely Wretch, that stab'd and ne'er repented !
Ah, minds of men, that read the things you see
Not as they are, but as you want them painted !
Ah, wild and beautiful, wert thou not free
To roam all space by mortals unfrequented ?

Latmos

About her waist his arm ; lips brush her cheek ;
His words beat on her—yet she does not speak.
She rests and lets him sob his soul away,
But her curl'd lips straighten them and grow bleak,
And in her eyes the fell and steely grey
Hardens like wintry dawns. His words grow weak.

Stammering he stands before her with bent head,
Rogue all confest. Her chill eyes freeze him dead.
No word she speaks, but cuts him to the bone
With that cold glitter. Under nameless dread
A shuddering takes him—his heart like a stone
Lies clog'd and lumpish with a weight of lead.

She has the power to slay him where he stands,
She has the will in her two clencht-up hands.
Swifter than lightning-flare her hissing word
Sears sinful flesh as with indelible brands—
Proclaims to Time Actæon red and scored,
And stricken Niobe weeping her bare lands.

Mere death were ease to such a drawn-out pain ;
He never knew her less than in this vein
Haggard and brooding, spiriting down ill
To hatch his ruin. Hot on him as rain
Fell thought of those sweet hours when they sat still
(He nursing what she suffer'd) : so his brain

Urged brokenly upon him what to plead
In voice made thick with tears. She had no heed
Of how he fell before her, claspt her knees,

Spilling desire even as his heart did bleed.
He calls her by the name she taught ; she sees
Nothing of him, his urgency or need.

Then he grew angry—Forsooth ! here was a girl
Spoilt by much love. He call'd her Spitfire, Churl ;
Bade her go sulk alone, to be asham'd ;
Prophesied her beseeching him a curl
For token, scorn'd her, stood with face inflam'd,
As sovereign men their wrath on women hurl.

'Take off (said he) to other lads your graces,
'Your wilful freaks, your airs and sour grimaces !
'Think you I cling to beauty in a pet ?
'I choose not play with girls of sullen faces.
'Get to your mother's lap, she'll ease your fret ;
'Then when you're meeker we may run more races.'

She laught a little. It was like the sound
Of a brook running, when the air is crown'd
With ripples and the plashy murmuring
Caught on March morns. Her bright lips were unbound ;
Two little dimples ventur'd, as in Spring
The wood-buds coyly peer above the ground.

Tremulously and low her silver voice
Swam into speech to make all earth rejoice—
A silver bell, the sighing of a flute
Made no more holy, or more delicate noise.
Endymion caught his breath and listen'd mute :—
She spoke, with warning finger held at poise.

Latmos

‘How wise it was of you to spoil our joy,
‘Endymion (thus she scolded), with annoy
‘Of mortal usage underneath the moon
‘That is so white she cannot be decoy
‘Of maidens from their treasure. All too soon
‘I rue my kindness, stooping to a boy.’

With that her pure throat let a little moan
That she was made so fair, that all alone
Her way must be, until in mortal man
That grace of God be given to look upon
Beauty for what it is, not what it can
Give unto us for sop to batten on.

So she with light upon her like a wreath
Of stars sped on her way with undim’d breath.
One little sigh she suffer’d, such as Gods
May know, who watch our footsteps far beneath
Their skyey thrones—envying our abodes,
Envying our lives of love, perhaps our death.

Envoy

The story saith there is a valley deep
And quiet in Dis, whereby the dead folk creep
On tiptoe, fearful lest some slipt-out groan
Should wake the sleeper out of his long sleep ;
But he wakes never. ’Tis Endymion,
Dreaming of Hymnia’s nightly fellowship.

And still by one long watcher of the night
Hymnia is seen, whenas the moon shines bright.
Across Taygetus she with her maids
Goes shiningly ; you know her by her height
And by her head borne queenly : on the glades
Men say she sheds the dew. But let him write

Who knows her best ; thus only goes his pray'r,
That she withdraw not from him, but still spare
Some little hint of beauty deep and calm
To cool his fever. He has no further care
What other fortune fall him, so the psalm
Incarnate in her, shrill as mountain air,

Fan her young breath upon him as she flits
Across him, looking downward where he sits ;
Or with grave beckoning in her solemn eyes
Bid him to follow far off, as befits
Attendant on her. *She* knoweth it he tries
To honour her with what he has of wits.

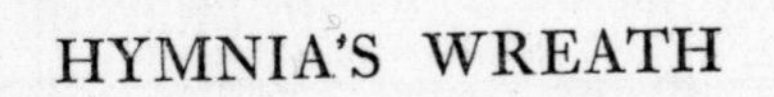

HYMNIA'S WREATH

AGROTERA

O'ER the long hills of folded Arcady
Fleets Artemis a-hunting of the deer,
Voiceth the shrill wind, and with eager cheer
Houndeth the laggard hounds to victory.
With hair let wild, green-kirtled to the knee,
Bare-throated, of high courage, supremely clear,
She is the captain, she the holy fere
Of all our world's immanent sanctity.
For when before some vile imputed thought
Standeth an untried soul, and leaps the sin,
Truth's candid girdle splintereth all to nought
The bloat offence ; and leaveth truth to win
Forth from her garner a shaft of Good untaught,
Which flares to the monstrous hide, and quivereth in.

HECATE

HECATE in the pauses of the night
Stealeth adown her silver-pavèd stair,
And draweth close, so from her fragrant hair
Mysterious potence issueth, and delight.
Then thro' the hush I feel her soul in flight
Beating wide wings about me, and all the air
Throb with her intimacy ; and lay me bare
Its secret, as to one that claims by right.
Then, knowing all her might, I fall to cower,
And worship, saying—Depart not Thou from me !
For all I have is Thine ; and in this hour
No lurking sense of mine is hid from Thee :
For lo ! I am Earth's, and Earth is all Thy power
And burns on Thy white brow, still Hecatè !

ORTHIA

Some native proud reserve she doth possess,
She that is Goddess of the limber spear :
Quiet possession, wrought of soberness
And the aloofness of her lunar sphere.
Half is her gravity of maiden stress,
Youth pricking youth, youth shrinking back for fear;
And half she weareth as the secure dress
Of sovranty indomitable-clear.
For, see, a Virgin Queen she doth appear
What time she rideth silver-cold the press
Of pallid stars, that shiver, yet draw near,
Courting the sweet disease of abjectness.
So dare not I her rooted pride abate,
Nor flout on Earth her more than human state.

ACTÆON

Men tell it whispering, Lady Artemis,
Cooling her sacred limbs at flood of noon,
Was of a hunter winded and spied. So soon
The clear-soul'd Virgin knew his hideousness,
She stood erect and shaking ; so, ere one hiss
Of terror bared the snake in mannish tune,
Shot a keen shaft upon him : he fell prone,
With all his clotted sin known as it is.
So I, when one unworthy thought at bay
Fell at the clear amazement of grey eyes,
Stood dog-like all confest, a sport, a prey
To that same earth which, bearing her, I prize.
Yet had I rather be a dog below her,
Spurn'd by her slim, proud feet, than never know her.

GLAUCOPIS

Not all the burnt-gold splendour of Southern eyes,
Nor that black hungry void of eyes that stare,
Nor the steel-flicker borrow'd from chill skies,
Are hers, that is the queen of Earth and Air.
But strangely interwoven mysteries—
Mysterious amethyst, and that hot vair
That sleeps in quiet lagoons and orient seas,
And violet-film as of soft evenings there—
Lo you ! the blended harmonies I read
Within her steadfast immemorial gazing ;
And sometimes wonder beacons, sometimes need,
But always candour, limpid past erasing.
Sometimes she is sad and tears do well and hover,
And take their tincture from, and fall to love her.

ENDYMION

SINCE you are silvern light-foot Artemis,
Then I must be the Latmian wandering wild,
Untam'd, unletter'd in honesty, beguiled
By frenzy's buffet-blast and passion's kiss.
Long time, as he, I whirl'd in the abyss
Of strife surging about me, that defiled
The stream of my life's issue ; nor once smiled
Good hope on me, till waking I was wis
Of some glad quiet Presence shed from far
Dim heights of vaulted skyey saphirine,
Some limpid candour, as of sudden star,
Spied when the sun-shot sky faints out in green ;
And was where Peace and high Possession are :
And all I might be stunned what I had been.

BOËDROMIOS

One came, love-bidden, and toucht me on the brow
With healing fingers ; I paled, but dared not look,
Yet whispered—In the volume of the book
'Tis written, Lady, I do thy work, and vow
To thee my song and service, that all men know
What spherèd soul came down and undertook
Ransome of tortur'd souls. So said, I shook
With her intol'rable mastery, and shake now.
For in her cool caressing finger-tips
Lay that which made me quiver and turn about
To babble my own sickness. Her immortal
And lambent fiery strength burst ope the portal :
Vistas amazing of realm on realm stretcht out !
I bow'd and went my way with sober'd lips.

KALLIGENEIA

Long waste of fever-days I paid my court
To that hot Queen of passionate abode
Deep in the green heart of our Earth, whence flow'd
As bountiful milk, meseemèd, every sort
Of eager cleaving ; in whose languorous port,
In whose faint sweetness I bathed deep my blood—
Genetrix, hailing her, Parent of Good
And Ill alike, God, and a God's consort !
  Then arose One and lookt on me ; most sad,
Most young ; slim of her years, of stature slight,
With haunting eyes ; whose pure, most sorrowful mouth
Quiver'd for eagerness in leash. She had,
For one long look, my service day and night :
'For I am Life,' it said, 'and God, and Youth !'

EUKLEIA

Queen of the white exalted lucent brow,
Sister of God, Mother of God in Man ;
Thronèd apart, still, cold as summit-snow,
Inflexibly chaste ; whose far-set eyes do scan
Earth and its toil from the live upper air ;
Whose pleasure only is the hard-kept vow,
Hard-won repression ; whose home is in the fair
Heart of a Virgin—hear us, and hasten thou !
Ah, clean and driven-white my soul is now ;
Clean, driven-white, since dying in thy flame,
I died, but lived indeed to turn the plough
Thro' past abominable fields of shame ;
Which throughly purged shall garner all seeds that grow
Meet for thy sickle, our Lady of Fair Fame !

TRIBUTE

ARTEMISION

Now Winter stealeth out like a white nun,
  Cloaking her face behind her icy fingers,
And men each day look longer at the Sun,
  While late and later yet the sweet light lingers.

Fast by the hedgerows, bit by gales of March,
  A chaplet for thy brows of delicate leaves—
Tendrils of briony, ruby tufts of larch,
  Woodsorrel, crocus pale, the New Year weaves.

Yet is thy smile half wintry, as forlorn
  To view thy state too solemn for thy years,
And half amazèd as a flower's, late born,
  And not more quick for pleasure than for tears.

Thy month austere telleth thy cloistral fashion :
March frost thy pride is, March wind thy pent passion.

SAINT BEAUTY

'*Or pensa quanta bellezza avea. . . . che nessuno che la vedesse mai la guardò per concupiscenza, tanto era la santità che rilustrava in lei.*'—SAVONAROLA.

IN chamber thought my mind is like a fire
  Kindled and set to roar by a strong wind,
  And my tongue eloquent, and my eyes blind
To all but mad pursuit of their desire.
But I am mute before thee, as a quire
  Of singers when one chant soars unconfin'd
  From one gold-throated minstrel: thou dost bind
My lips, eyes, heart, my very thought's attire

For body's beauty is thy soul's thin veil
  Wherethro' soul's beauty shineth like a jewel
    Blood-bright, whose too pure strength would else assail
Earth-groping eyes: it hath thy soul's impress,
  It hath thy soul's white magic, but, less cruel,
    Soul's pride softened by body's courteousness.

EROS NARCISSUS

If I should force the sentries of her lips,
  What should it profit me, to shock her soul?
Or see young Faith in pitiful eclipse,
  Or watch her don Abasement's leaden stole?

If I should bid her tell me all her love,
  Bare all the rosy secret of her heart;
What gain, to see her spoil herself thereof?
  For her what gain, to see her love depart?

Her lovely mystery is her loveliness,
  And her sweet reticence her seal of price;
For what she loveth darkly that she is—
  Priestess, communicant, and sacrifice.

In her own mould she fashions Love, and he
Scarce knows himself, vested so tenderly.

THAT STONE WALLS CAN NEVER SEPARATE HIM FROM HIS LADY

NEVER the shadow of a summer cloud
  Can fleet between my lady and my loving ;
The miser World shall find my head unbow'd
  And my heart's temper high beyond its proving.

My heart is fixt to be her Prisoner,
  And she, an honest Janitress, the keys
Doth shrine in her own heart as Treasurer,
  So sure that Death itself were not Decease.

For if upon a day Fate proved unkind
  And grimly stalkt betwixt my Love and me,
The glancing motions of her faithful mind
  Would glint athwart him plain for me to see ;

And in her beamy light above his shroud
I'd see her smile, gay, confident and proud.

HIS LADY A THIEF

THAT intercourse with thee I have in dreams
But serves to whet my anguish to be reft,
Not of thy sight which visits me in gleams,
But of my consciousness of thy sweet theft.

Thou wert the thief of me, and I, the thiev'd,
Felt such great riches viewing thee in act
To rob me daily, nothing less I griev'd
Than being accessory to thy fact.

Now by a forced decree love to the lover
Is render'd back, it hath no further use
Than stare reproach at him who gave it over,
And lookt to gain by so much he did lose.

O my blest thief, come rifle all my treasure;
I cannot love but only out of measure!

RITUAL

PREPARATION

I ARISE to anoint my soul
With the unction of her sweet breath,
To bathe and wash in the light
Of her eyes clearer than snow.
Her eyes are like hyacinth,
And deep as the sea, and dark
As the hold of the mountain water.
To-day, in an hour, she and I
Will be face to face : from her eyes
Her startled soul will look out,
And mine will be comforted
To lend comfort to hers.

Ah, Saint Lucy, whose light
Ceased not with breath, nor was quencht
Under the knife-edge ! Now
With the scars heal'd you are come,
Stoopt from heaven to earth :
And your eyes kindle and burn,
Gleam insurgent, are dewy
Like April blotted in tears,
Or quick to the Sun. Laugh now !
Laugh now, let no crying
Beat at your heart's shut door
For the treasure hidden and held.

Ritual

Ah, little Maid!
Ah, little Queen, crown'd and raised up above,
Are you afraid?
Are you tremulous, fearing the accolade
Of my singing of love?
The flutter'd heart of a bird
Throbs thro' his wing; your heart
Cries in your pitiful mouth,
In your wide eyes, in your meek
Hands folded and still!
Give me your two hands—so; let me hold them and kneel
Till the tempest be done,
And the sun shine over your face.

'DONNA È GENTIL—'

THY lonely virginal air,
And thy vague eyes,
The carven stillness of thy sorrowful mouth
And sanctity of thy youth,
Mark thee for no man's prize:
Set thee apart to be fair,
Holy, lovely, and wise.

Being so fair thou art holy
Even as Beatrice is:
Sister-torches of God,
Twin pastures untrod,
Handmaidens meek and lowly,
Consecrate priestesses,
To Heaven dedicate wholly.

Thy face drinketh the light;
Moon-lit, girdled with stars,
Sapphire-gemm'd and adorn'd,
Thou art that lamp which burn'd,
From the beginning! The bars
Of Wisdom were overturn'd:
Innocence claim'd her birthright.

Ritual

In the clear spaces of Heaven,
As sisters and lovers sit
Beatrice and Thou embraced,
Hand and hand, waist and waist,
And smile at the worship given
By earth, and the men in it
To whom you were manifest.

And because I have loved you well,
And because I was born for this
(As the great Tuscan was born
To love and serve Beatrice),
I, who have suffer'd all scorn,
Spend my treasure to tell
Your high worthiness.

ROSA NASCOSA

MORE than those
Enfranchised beauties her perfection shows,
Like a concealèd rose,
But to the thickets where she lieth close.

These libertines
Encompass her with hardy-visaged spines ;
She frets not nor repines,
But does their bidding meekly, and resigns

Herself to be
Their bond-servant, who shall be more than free ;
Having a liberty
There where her soul can fear no enemy.

There she doth find
All broad dominion and a heaven all kind,
In her unravisht mind
Whereto her brute possessioners are blind.

Possession goes
No deeper than the surface ; there are mines
Far down, whose sacred fee
And golden hold no trammelling can bind.

SONGS OF OCCASIONS

TO CROCUSES

I ASK you not, frail crocuses, that set
Light wings and thin
Alert to air still sharp with winter fret,
Bestow your innocence for coronet
On me, struck deep in sin ;
Yet suffer me to win
So much of outlook sober and demure
As yours, and pure,
That with your flush my spring-time may begin.

Whether upon the grass kirtled in white
(Snow-drifted thither),
Or one by one, yet lingering and slight,
Your little fires broider a linkèd light,
And beacon in black weather
The way for men, or whether,
More violet than heart of amethyst,
You kneel at rest
In folded peace, as nuns that pray together ;

Let my upspringing be as glacial-clean,
And let me stand

Rejoicing in the sun-washt deep demesne
With you and all young flowers fresh and keen
As new rain on the land ;
With you to lift up hand,
Shrilling my orison at break of day,
Then bowing, say—
'We come and go, live, die, at God's command.'

Yours are mute raptures, silent ecstasies,
The secret song
Of carven angel-brood whose litanies
Peal from wide-open eyes, and like lilies
Are blown in a throng,
By hidden wind and strong
About the fencèd garden, where the Maid
And Mother, having laid
To sleep her firstling, crooneth all day long.

O glad your coming, and your service glad,
Sweet-breathèd things !
You look not to the prison once you had
Take no thought wherewithal you shall be clad ;
You have no sorrowings,
Nor rankle of coward-stings ;
But spearing ever upwards in your flight
You strain to light,
Then listen clear-eyed till the chant begins.

If there is any music left in us,
Or any mirth

To Crocuses

Whose song may well from hearts made bounteous
As flows your still delight when, emulous,
Spring leaps from winter's dearth,
Let such an equal worth
Of quiet-hued deliciousness be ours,
That with your patient flowers
We fold on singing-robes to praise this goodly earth.

SONG

Ask me not how much I love you;
Be content!
If too much love were sin
You would but win
Some of my punishment.
Ask me not, but believe I merely love you.

If indeed I truly love you,
Never more
Will any harm come near,
Nor need you fear
My heart's voice at the door
Of your heart, whisp'ring, Open, sweet, I love you.

See! I cannot choose but love you
Soberly.
For, having felt your touch,
My pride in such
Familiarity
Warns me how he must worship who would love you.

A SONG FOR A LUTE AT NIGHT

I love only thee—
What is that to thee?
Royal youth goes careless,
Frank and flusht and tearless.
Royal youth is free:
Take no thought of me.

I love only thee—
What is that to thee?
Beauty must have servants,
If by my observance
I pay beauty's fee,
Take no thought for me.

I love only thee—
What is that to thee?
If thou wert compassionate,
Courteous, I might fashion it
Into more—Let be:
Take no thought of me.

I love only thee—
What is that to thee?
This! Like apple-blossom
Wind-swept is thy bosom

When thou seest me
Taking thought of thee.

This it is to thee !
All my love of thee
Holds thy breath and sways it
Like a lute, and plays it :
And the melody
Is thy thought of me.

Keep thy thought of me
Shyly, secretly.
I ask not to know it
More than thou dost show it
When thy colours flee
Chasing over thee.

Never thine for me.
As my love for thee !
Daily to go aching,
Nightly to lie waking ;
Restless as the sea.
Long not so for me.

IN A CHURCH

HE : How comes it you can bend so proud a head,
Or still to quietness a heart so wild?

SHE : God asketh of us in return for bread
That we bow down ; and I would be His child.

HE : Why do you move your lips so brokenly ;
Your hands, why fold them crosswise on your heart?

SHE : My poor lips dare not ask outspokenly,
And for my hands, theirs is the suppliant part.

HE : Dare you not turn the glory of your eyes
Upward to Him? Why must they be downcast?
Is it lest they should dim the very skies?

SHE : I look to raise them up to God at last.

HE : Are you a nun, to veil your shining hair?
What is this meekness lulling your clear voice?

SHE : Women may not approach Him with heads bare,
Nor will He have His House defiled with noise.

HE : Do you love God so hardly that salt tears
Gleam on your cheeks and drop upon your breast?

SHE : The world is hard for me and full of fears,
And He saith, Come and I will give you rest.
I pray for that.

HE : What paltering is this ;
When I stand here——

SHE : O hush ! This is God's place.
Go now.

HE : You bow your head the Rood to kiss :
And I have never kiss'd your sorrowful face.
Speak ! Do you know I love you ?

SHE : It is sin.
You must not love me. That is why I pray.

HE : That I should cease to love you ?

SHE : That you win
Enough of grace to dare to go away.

HE : You are my Saint !

SHE : Alas ! no Saint am I.

HE : Why do you hold your heart so close ?

SHE : It aches.

HE : And I must leave you aching ?

SHE : Yes. Good-bye.

HE : Why do you hold your heart ?

SHE : For fear it breaks.

Everything in this book was composed between 1895 *and* 1898. *The Dedication and some of the short poems are reprinted from a book of verse called 'Songs and Meditations,' which was published in* 1896 *and expired painlessly within a little time of birth. They are reproduced because they belong to the subject of the present issue. The three long poems have never been printed before; nor have the Sonnets grouped together as Hymnia's Wreath.*

Perhaps I may be excused for adding that the intended musical effect of such poems as the Dedication, 'Preparation,' and 'Donna è gentil—' can only be got by reading them as if they were written in prose. The natural stresses will then fall into their places in the scheme.

London, February, 1909.

LONDON:
PRINTED BY WILLIAM CLOWES AND SONS, LIMITED.